FINANCIAL POST

FPbonds
Government

Additional Publications

For more detailed information or to place an order, see the back of the book.

CANADIAN ALMANAC & DIRECTORY 2025
Répetoire et almanach canadien
2,348 pages, 8 ½ x 11, Hardcover
178th edition, December 2024
ISBN 978-1-63700-912-3
ISSN 0068-8193
A combination of textual material, charts, colour photographs and directory listings, the *Canadian Almanac & Directory* provides the most comprehensive picture of Canada, from physical attributes to economic and business summaries to leisure and recreation.

CANADIAN WHO'S WHO 2025
1,200 pages, 8 3/8 x 10 7/8, Hardcover
December 2024
ISBN 978-1-63700-922-2
ISSN 0068-9963
Published for over 100 years, this authoritative annual publication offers access to the top 10,000 notable Canadians in all walks of life, including details such as date and place of birth, education, family details, career information, memberships, creative works, honours, languages, and awards, together with full addresses. Included are outstanding Canadians from business, academia, politics, sports, the arts and sciences, and more, selected because of the positions they hold in Canadian society, or because of the contributions they have made to Canada.

FINANCIAL POST DIRECTORY OF DIRECTORS 2025
Répertoire des administrateurs
1,751 pages, 5 7/8 x 9, Hardcover
78th edition, September 2024
ISBN 978-1-63700-924-6
ISSN 0071-5042
Published biennially and annually since 1931, this comprehensive resource offers readers access to approximately 16,600 executive contacts from Canada's top 1,400 corporations. The directory provides a definitive list of directorships and offices held by noteworthy Canadian business people, as well as details on prominent Canadian companies (both public and private), including company name, contact information and the names of executive officers and directors. Includes all-new front matter and three indexes.

CANADIAN PARLIAMENTARY GUIDE 2025
Guide parlementaire canadien
1,310 pages, 6 x 9, Hardcover
159th edition, April 2025
ISBN 979-8-89179-345-3
ISSN 0315-6168
Published annually since before Confederation, this indispensable guide to government in Canada provides information on federal and provincial governments, with biographical sketches of government members, descriptions of government institutions, and historical text and charts. With significant bilingual sections, the Guide covers elections from Confederation to the present, including the most recent provincial elections.

ASSOCIATIONS CANADA 2025
Associations du Canada
2,130 pages, 8 ½ x 11, Softcover
46th edition, February 2025
ISBN 979-8-89179-341-5
ISSN 1484-2408
Over 20,200 entries profile Canadian and international organizations active in Canada. Over 2,000 subject classifications index activities, professions and interests served by associations. Includes listings of NGOs, institutes, coalitions, social agencies, federations, foundations, trade unions, fraternal orders, and political parties. Fully indexed by subject, acronym, budget, conference, executive name, geographic location, mailing list availability, and registered charitable organization.

FINANCIAL SERVICES CANADA 2025-2026
Services financiers au Canada
1,500 pages, 8 ½ x 11, Softcover
26th edition, June 2025
ISBN 979-8-89179-343-9
ISSN 1484-2408
This directory of Canadian financial institutions and organizations includes banks and depository institutions, non-depository institutions, investment management firms, financial planners, insurance companies, accountants, major law firms, associations, and financial technology companies. Fully indexed.

MAJOR CANADIAN CITIES: COMPARED & RANKED
Comparaison et classement des principales villes canadiennes
1,372 pages, 8 ½ x 11, Softcover
2nd edition, January 2024
ISBN 978-8-89179-049-0
This second edition of *Major Canadian Cities: Compared and Ranked* has been completely revised with 2021 census data, including new tables and a refreshed layout. It provides an in-depth comparison and analysis of the 50 most populated cities in Canada. Each chapter incorporates information from dozens of resources to create the following major sections: Background, Study Rankings, and Statistical Tables.

LIBRARIES CANADA 2023-2024
Bibliothèques Canada
900 pages, 8 ½ x 11, Softcover
37th edition, July 2023
ISBN 978-1-67300-690-0
ISSN 1920-2849
Libraries Canada offers comprehensive information on Canadian libraries, resource centres, business information centres, professional associations, regional library systems, archives, library schools, government libraries, and library technical programs.

FINANCIAL POST

FPbonds
Government
2025

Grey House Publishing Canada
PUBLISHER: Leslie Mackenzie
GENERAL MANAGER: Bryon Moore

Grey House Publishing
EDITORIAL DIRECTOR: Stuart Paterson
SENIOR VICE PRESIDENT, MARKETING: Jessica Moody

Grey House Publishing Canada
3 – 1500 Upper Middle Road
PO Box 76017
Oakville, ON **L6M 3H5**
866-433-4739
FAX 416-644-1904
www.greyhouse.ca
e-mail: info@greyhouse.ca

Grey House Publishing Canada Inc. is a wholly owned subsidiary of Grey House Publishing Inc. USA.

While every effort has been made to ensure the reliability of the information presented in this publication, Grey House Publishing Canada Inc. and Postmedia Network Inc. neither guarantees the accuracy of the data contained herein nor assumes any responsibility for errors, omissions or discrepancies.

Errors brought to the attention of the publisher and verified to the satisfaction of the publisher will be corrected in future editions.

Except by express prior written permission of the Copyright Proprietor no part of this work may be copied by any means of publication or communication now known or developed hereafter including, but not limited to, use in any compilation or other print or electronic publication, in any information storage and retrieval system, in any other electronic device, or in any visual or audio-visual device or product or internet product.

This publication is an original and creative work, copyrighted by Postmedia Network Inc. and Grey House Publishing Canada Inc. and is fully protected by all applicable copyright laws, as well as by laws covering misappropriation, trade secrets and unfair competition.

Grey House Publishing Canada Inc. has added value to the underlying factual material through one or more of the following efforts: unique and original selection; expression; arrangement; coordination; and classification.

Postmedia Network Inc. and Grey House Publishing Inc. will defend their rights in this publication.

© 2025, Postmedia Network Inc.
365 Bloor St. East
Toronto, ON M4W 3L4
Email: fpadvisor@postmedia.com
legacy-fpadvisor.financialpost.com

Text © 2025 by Postmedia Network Inc.
Texte © 2025 par Postmedia Network Inc.
Cover, Front Matter and Back Matter © 2025 by Grey House Publishing Canada Inc.
Couverture, matière première et publicités de produits © 2025 par Grey House Publishing Canada Inc.

Published in print form by Grey House Publishing Canada Inc. under exclusive license from Postmedia Network Inc. All rights reserved.
Publié sous forme imprimé par Grey House Publishing Canada Inc. sous licence exclusive de Postmedia Network Inc. Tous droits réservés.

Printed in Canada by Marquis Book Printing Inc.

ISSN: 1486-7273
ISBN: 979-8-89179-361-3

Cataloguing in Publication Data is available from Libraries and Archives Canada.

Contents

ASSESSING THE IMPACT OF THE BANK OF CANADA'S GOVERNMENT BOND PURCHASES vii
A look at the Bank of Canada's use of quantitative easing (QE) during the COVID-19 pandemic and its repercussions.

COULD ALL-TO-ALL TRADING IMPROVE LIQUIDITY IN THE GOVERNMENT OF CANADA BOND MARKET? xxxv
A theoretical look at adopting an all-to-all market structure to improve the resilience of government bond markets during periods of turmoil.

HOW FOREIGN CENTRAL BANKS CAN AFFECT LIQUIDITY IN THE GOVERNMENT OF CANADA BOND MARKET xlv
An examination of the trading behaviour of foreign central banks and its potential impact on liquidity in the Government of Canada bond market.

INTRODUCTION 1
Description of the contents of the book.

PROVINCIAL UNDERWRITERS 2
List of underwriting managers by province.

CANADIAN TAXATION 3
Outline of the various tax levies in Canada that affect investments in debt obligations of or guaranteed by the Canadian Federal or Provincial Governments.

CANADA 9
Statistical overview of the country.

DIRECT DEBT 10
Table of Government of Canada direct debt, listed by maturity date.

GUARANTEED DEBT 11
Table of Government of Canada guaranteed debt, listed alphabetically by government agency.

CALLABLE BONDS 14
Table of Government of Canada callable bonds, listed alphabetically by government agency.

TREASURY BILLS 15
Table of Treasury Bills, listed by maturity date.

ALBERTA 19
Tables of direct and guaranteed debt following a statistical overview of the province.

BRITISH COLUMBIA 22
Table of direct debt following a statistical overview of the province.

MANITOBA 25
Table of direct debt following a statistical overview of the province.

NEW BRUNSWICK 29
Tables of direct and guaranteed debt following a statistical overview of the province.

NEWFOUNDLAND AND LABRADOR 32
Tables of direct and guaranteed debt following a statistical overview of the province.

NOVA SCOTIA 35
   Tables of direct and guaranteed debt following a statistical overview of the province.

ONTARIO 37
   Tables of direct and guaranteed debt following a statistical overview of the province.

PRINCE EDWARD ISLAND 43
   Tables of direct and guaranteed debt following a statistical overview of the province.

QUÉBEC 45
   Tables of direct debt, guaranteed debt, and callable bonds following a statistical overview of the province.

SASKATCHEWAN 51
   Table of direct debt following a statistical overview of the province.

EUROBONDS 55
   Debt offered in the European market, listed alphabetically by government issuer.

BANK OF CANADA
BANQUE DU CANADA

Assessing the Impact of the Bank of Canada's Government Bond Purchases

Staff Discussion Paper 2024-5 (English)
Chinara Azizova, Jonathan Witmer, Xu Zhang
June 2024

Introduction

In the wake of the 2008–09 global financial crisis, several central banks introduced large-scale asset purchase programs, commonly referred to as quantitative easing (QE). The goal of these QE programs is to address financial market strains and to provide additional monetary stimulus once policy interest rates are at, or close to, their effective lower bounds. QE has therefore become an important tool used by many central banks around the world to affect monetary conditions once traditional interest rate tools are constrained. Although the Bank of Canada did not employ QE in response to the global financial crisis, QE is nonetheless part of the Bank's framework for conducting monetary policy at low interest rates (Bank of Canada 2015).

In March 2020, the Bank implemented a federal government bond purchase program to address the financial and economic strains caused by the COVID-19 pandemic. Known as the Government of Canada Bond Purchase Program (GBPP), it was introduced as the Bank lowered its policy interest rate to its lower bound of 25 basis points (bps).[1, 2] The program began by purchasing a minimum of $5 billion Government of Canada (GoC) securities in the secondary market each week. These purchases were financed by increasing the size of settlement balances (known as "reserves" in other jurisdictions).[3] The GBPP's stated goal at the time was "…to address strains in the GoC debt market and to enhance the effectiveness of all other actions taken so far…" (Poloz 2020a). The Bank committed to continuing its purchases "…until the economic recovery is well underway." As financial strains subsided, the purpose of the GBPP transitioned away from addressing financial strains. Instead, it became a tool to provide "…the necessary degree of monetary policy accommodation required to achieve the inflation target" (Bank of Canada 2020).

The pace of the Bank's QE program decreased as economic conditions improved:

- On October 28, 2020, the Bank recalibrated the QE program to shift purchases toward longer-term bonds and reduced the pace to at least $4 billion a week.
- On April 21, 2021, the Bank adjusted the weekly net purchases of GoC bonds to a target of $3 billion. This reduction in the amount of incremental stimulus being added each week reflected the progress made in Canada's economic recovery.
- On July 14, 2021, the target pace was adjusted to $2 billion per week.
- On October 27, 2021, the Bank ended quantitative easing and entered a reinvestment phase. During this phase, the purchase of GoC bonds was solely to replace maturing bonds so that the Bank's holdings remained relatively stable over time.
- On April 13, 2022, the Bank announced that it was ending its reinvestment phase and would begin the process of quantitative tightening (QT).

By the end of the reinvestment phase, the GBPP had purchased approximately $340 billion of government bonds with a weighted average maturity of about six years. To put the pace and scale of the Bank's asset purchase programs in perspective, **Chart 1** compares the Bank's balance sheet as a percentage of gross domestic product (GDP) with that of the Federal Reserve, the European Central Bank and the Bank of England. The chart highlights four notable observations:

- Unlike the other central banks, the Bank of Canada did not engage in QE following the global financial crisis. As a result, its balance sheet was much smaller than the balance sheets of the other central banks when the pandemic began.
- The pace of the Bank's asset purchases following the onset of the pandemic was faster than the pace of balance sheet expansion in other central banks, normalizing by GDP. However, although the pace was faster at the beginning of the pandemic, the total amount of the Bank's balance sheet expansion during the pandemic was smaller than that of the other central banks. In addition, much of the fast pace of the increase was due to lending operations; when we exclude those operations, the pace is similar.
- At its peak, the Bank's balance sheet, as a percentage of GDP, was about half the size of the comparable measure for the other central banks.
- The Bank's balance sheet has declined more than the others' since its peak, largely for two reasons:
    - Several assets the Bank purchased (including GBPP and non-GBPP assets) were short-term in nature and therefore matured soon after QT began.
    - The Bank wound down its lending operations, while those of the other central banks are ongoing.

Chart 1: Changes in components of central banks' balance sheets as a percentage of nominal GDP

a. Bank of Canada

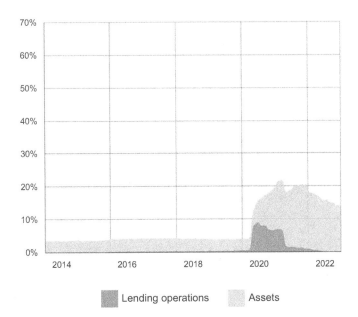

Lending operations　　Assets

b. Federal Reserve

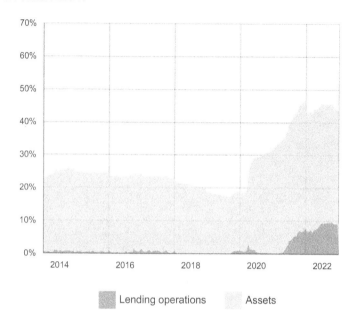

c. European Central Bank

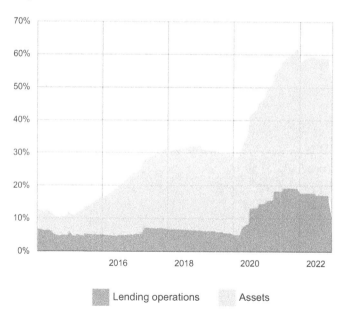

d. Bank of England

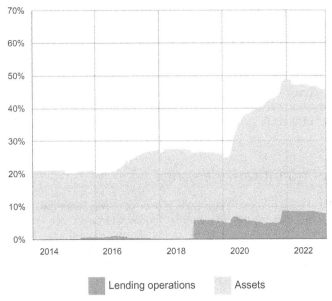

Sources: Board of Governors of the Federal Reserve System, European Central Bank, Bank of England and Bank of Canada
Last observation: December 2022

This was the first time the Bank used QE, and the amount needed during the pandemic was considerable. Therefore, it is crucial that we understand the impact of this monetary policy tool not only on financial markets but also on the economy. Johnson (2023) reviews all the Bank's market operations related to the pandemic and provides some recommendations on how their design and implementation could be changed in the future. Arora et al. (2021) analyze intraday movements in GoC bond yields in the hour after the Bank first announced the GBPP on March 27, 2020, at 9 a.m. They find that the announcement of the GBPP had a strong and immediate impact, with 10-year benchmark GoC bond yields declining by about 10 bps immediately after the announcement.

The rest of this paper is organized as follows. First, we extend Arora et al.'s (2021) evaluation of the financial market impact of the GBPP by:

- considering a larger set of GBPP-related announcements
- investigating the impact of the GBPP on a broader range of financial market assets

We find that, across a large set of announcements, 10-year bond yields declined by about 20 bps, with similar declines for other maturities. Since the impact of the GBPP is likely larger than the announcement-related returns, in a back-of-the-envelope counterfactual we estimate that the GBPP may have had an impact of almost 80 bps on 10-year bond yields.

Second, using Zhang's (2021) model, we use this counterfactual to estimate the impact of the GBPP on inflation and output.[4] With an 80 bps impact on 10-year bond yields, the model counterfactual suggests that the GBPP had a peak impact of about 3% on real GDP and 1.8 annualized percentage points on inflation. Meanwhile, a counterfactual with a 20 bps impact on 10-year bond yields suggests a peak impact of about 0.6% on real GDP and 0.6 annualized percentage points on inflation.

Theory of quantitative easing

The objective of QE is to support aggregate economic activity when the traditional instrument of monetary policy—the short-term nominal interest rate—cannot be reduced further because it is constrained by the effective lower bound. The general idea is that asset purchases can reduce longer-maturity interest rates while the overnight rate is near zero. From a theoretical perspective, there are three potential channels through which QE can impact financial market prices and the economy.

Signalling channel

In this channel, QE announcements signal to market participants that the central bank has changed its views on current or future economic conditions (Bauer and Rudebusch 2014). Alternatively, QE announcements may convey information about changes in the monetary policy reaction function or in policy objectives, such as the inflation target. In such cases, investors may alter their expectations for the future path of the policy rate, perhaps by lengthening the period they expect short-term interest rates to be near zero.[5] Sometimes, market participants anticipate a future path of interest rates based on the timing or implied sequencing of QE or QT. For example, if participants believe that the central bank will not raise the overnight rate from its lower bound until it stops QE or starts QT, then any announcement related to QE or QT can change expectations for interest rates.

Likewise, implied sequencing means that interest rate announcements can also influence expectations for QE. If participants expect QE to begin once the overnight rate approaches the lower bound, then rate cuts near the lower bound may increase their expectations for QE. This makes it challenging to measure the impact of QE, since participants may already have expectations for QE by the time the central bank officially announces a QE program.

Sometimes, QE announcements are accompanied by forward guidance announcements where the central bank "...provides direct information about the probable state of monetary policy in the future" (Sutherland 2023). In this sense, a central bank's QE program may be interpreted as a signal of its commitment to maintaining its forward guidance policy.

Portfolio balance channel

For this channel to be effective, financial markets need some friction or segmentation. Otherwise, QE purchases would be neutral and would have no impact on asset prices (Wallace 1981).[6] In effect, QE is the swap of one asset for another (Melzer 2010). The central bank removes government bonds from the market and replaces them with settlement balances (an asset for payment system participants). Under the assumption of complete and competitive markets, this asset swap should have no impact on asset prices. This is analogous to Ricardian equivalence (for debt versus taxes) and the theorem of Modigliani-Miller (for choice of financing structure of firms). The implication is that, in the absence of frictions or segmentation, the demand curve for long-term bonds would be flat.

Several types of models have introduced segmentation and frictions to demonstrate how QE can increase asset prices. Vayanos and Vila (2021) are often cited as a prime example of the portfolio balance channel. In their model, preferred-habitat investors invest only in bonds of a specific maturity (e.g., 10-year bonds). In addition, risk-averse arbitrageurs may invest across the entire maturity spectrum. In doing so, they are exposed to duration risk—the risk that interest rates will change. Since they are risk averse, they require compensation for bearing that risk in the form of a term premium on longer-term bonds. In Vayanos and Vila's (2021) model, QE removes duration risk from the market and reduces the risk exposure of arbitrageurs, thus reducing the term premium on all bonds. The impact of QE is stronger when arbitrageurs are more risk averse. Indeed, in their model, QE would have no impact if arbitrageurs were risk neutral.

Several other factors may influence the effectiveness of the portfolio balance channel of QE. For instance, if interest rates are near their lower bound and are expected to remain there for an extended period, there is less duration risk in the market and the impact of QE may be smaller (King 2019). As well, the impact of QE may be smaller in a small open economy if there is a high degree of substitutability between domestic and foreign assets (Kabaca 2016; Diez de los Rios and Shamloo 2017).

To put this theory in perspective, **Chart 2** illustrates how the Bank of Canada's QE changed the portfolio holdings of market participants. Given the fiscal policy response to support households and businesses at the onset of the pandemic, there was a sharp increase in the gross quantity of government bonds outstanding, especially bonds with less than five years of maturity. Absent QE, the portfolio balance theory suggests that this increase in government bonds outstanding would have increased both duration risk in the market and the term premium on government bonds. **Chart 2** also shows that the Bank's QE absorbed most of this increase in the gross supply of government bonds outstanding. The fiscal policy response and the Bank's QE were reacting to the same worrisome economic and financial conditions, which is why government debt and QE both increased at the same time. However, because of the Bank's QE, the market did not need to absorb the extra duration risk from the government's issuance. If the market had had to absorb this extra risk, arbitrageurs would have demanded more compensation to hold long-term bonds, which means that the term premium would have been higher.

Chart 2: Ownership of Government of Canada bonds

a. Bonds with terms of 5 years or less

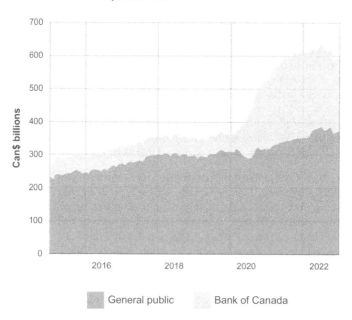

b. Bonds with terms longer than 5 years

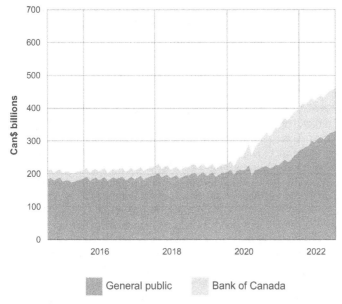

Source: Bank of Canada
Last observation: January 31, 2023

Liquidity channel or market functioning channel

QE purchases can increase asset prices by reducing the liquidity risk premium. This premium results in a higher yield and compensates investors for the risk that they would have to prematurely liquidate their long position in a security at an unfavourable price. Unlike the portfolio balance channel, in which QE impacts prices upon announcement, in the liquidity channel, prices (and liquidity metrics) generally move when the QE purchases are made (Vissing-Jorgensen 2021).

QE can help restore market functioning when the capacity of dealers to intermediate in the market is impaired and causes the liquidity risk premium to rise abruptly (Duffie and Keane 2023). Large-scale asset purchases for market functioning can occur even when the overnight rate is not at its lower bound. Duffie and Keane (2023) point out that, although monetary policy and market functioning goals are usually well aligned, this is not always the case. For example, in autumn 2022 the Bank of England purchased gilts at the same time that it was tightening monetary policy.

Christensen and Gillan (2022) posit that the liquidity risk premium is the result of a bargaining game between buyers and sellers, and that large-scale asset purchases increase the bargaining power of sellers by providing a committed buyer. They argue that this increase in bargaining power increases the price and thus lowers the yield of the bond (i.e., it reduces the liquidity risk premium) because those selling are less likely to be squeezed.

Transmission of quantitative easing

The ultimate goal of QE is to stimulate broader economic activity to help achieve the inflation target. **Figure 1** illustrates how QE may transmit to the broader economy. In the first step of the transmission, all three channels increase financial market prices and reduce yields. Each channel may impact a different set of financial market prices. The signalling channel is more likely to have a greater impact on bonds with shorter maturities (i.e., less than two or three years). The portfolio balance channel, meanwhile, may have a greater impact on longer-maturity bonds when the central bank removes duration risk. QE may also impact the specific bonds being purchased if it helps to restore market liquidity. QE purchases not only increase the price of government bonds but also influence the prices of other assets, such as foreign bonds, corporate bonds and foreign exchange (e.g., Neely 2015; Diez de los Rios and Shamloo 2017; Krishnamurthy and Vissing-Jorgensen 2011). This rise in asset prices increases wealth and reduces borrowing costs for both households and firms. In turn, households and firms increase their investment and consumption, raising both GDP and inflation.

Figure 1: Stylized transmission of quantitative easing

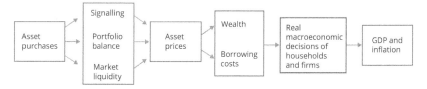

It becomes more difficult to measure its impact as QE moves further along the transmission path. Changes in financial market prices in a short window around QE announcements can easily be observed, but the same cannot be said for changes in macroeconomic variables. Macroeconomic variables are reported less frequently (e.g., monthly or quarterly), and inflation and GDP respond to monetary policy with a lag. One approach to measuring the impact of QE on macroeconomic variables is to include asset purchases in a vector autoregression (VAR) model with sign and zero restrictions (e.g., Weale and Wieladeck 2022). Another approach is to incorporate financial market frictions directly into a dynamic stochastic general equilibrium (DSGE) model (e.g., Chen, Cúrdia and Ferrero 2012). As above, there is a risk with empirical work that estimates are averages of different state-dependent effects at different times. In DSGE models, a risk is that estimation or calibration is primarily reflective of "normal times" and that in periods of Knightian uncertainty, estimates could have particularly large error bands.

Financial market impact

At least two main challenges make measuring the impact of QE on financial markets difficult. First, understanding the impact of QE on government bond yields requires understanding the slope of the demand curve for long-term government bonds. That is, how much does a change in the quantity of government bonds impact the yield that the market demands to hold those bonds? The challenge is that the slope of the demand curve is not easily observed and likely not constant. The slope may be relatively flat when the outstanding quantity of bonds is moderate but become steeper when the quantity of bonds grows. Moreover, this demand curve may shift over time and become steeper in times of financial stress and increasing risk aversion. Krishnamurthy and Vissing-Jorgensen (2012), for instance, examine the aggregate demand curve for US Treasury debt and show that it does not have a constant slope. Further, in an update on his website, Krishnamurthy shows that this demand curve has shifted since the global financial crisis due to an increase in demand for safe assets.

Second, to understand the full impact of QE on financial markets, we need to understand the counterfactual scenario of how financial market prices would have evolved without QE. The effect of QE is the difference between actual prices and prices in this counterfactual scenario. Since this counterfactual scenario cannot be observed, most studies quantify the impact of QE on financial market prices by measuring how those prices respond to QE announcements made by the central bank. Measuring QE using this approach assumes that financial market prices just before the announcement are a good approximation of the counterfactual scenario of no QE. This implies that QE was completely unexpected, since financial market prices should reflect the market's expectations for QE.

For example, it is unlikely that the GBPP was completely unexpected when the Bank first announced it, given that other countries had previously introduced QE programs, and given that the overnight rate had already been moved toward its lower bound. Further, market participants probably formed expectations about the size of the GBPP after these announcements were made. For instance, it may be the case that as long as purchases were being made (especially in the early period when the Bank was purchasing at least $5 billion per week), market participants were increasing their expectations for the duration (and hence the overall size) of the GBPP.

Figure 2 illustrates these challenges in a supply and demand framework. In this framework, the demand curve slopes upward since we are examining yields and not prices. Suppose that, before the pandemic, the supply of bonds is given by the vertical supply curve S_A. The equilibrium bond yield is given by its level at point A in the diagram. Given the pandemic programs, the market expects the government to expand supply so that the supply curve moves to the right to curve S_B. In the absence of any other measures, bond yields increase to the level at point B in the diagram. However, because market participants also expect that there is a high probability the central bank will implement a QE program that will offset some of this supply, the expected supply curve does not shift to curve S_B but instead shifts to curve S_C. So, we do not observe yields at the level at point B in the diagram, but only observe yields at the level at point C. Once the central bank officially announces a QE program, expectations for supply shift to the left to curve S_D.

The impact of QE we are interested in measuring is the difference between the counterfactual yields when there is no QE and the actual yields. In **Figure 2**, this means we are interested in the difference between the yields at point B and the yields at point D. Unfortunately, when we measure the yield changes around QE announcements, we measure only the difference between yields at point C and yields at point D. Further, it is a challenge to extrapolate the announcement impact to get the full impact because:

- We don't know how much markets changed their expectation of QE when the announcement was made.
- The slope of the yield curve likely changes, so extrapolating from the flatter (steeper) part of the demand curve may underestimate (overestimate) the impact.

Figure 2: Illustrative supply and demand for long-term bonds

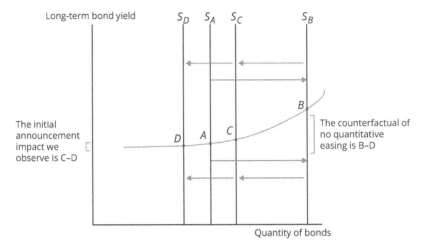

We employ three strategies to mitigate these challenges, each with advantages and disadvantages. In our first strategy, we examine changes in long-term bond yields that occurred around a much broader set of Bank of Canada communications, including some announcements before the Bank officially announced its QE program. These communications include not only our interest rate announcements but also speeches made by Governing Council members and reports on results of operations. This strategy is not perfect:

- Market expectations may still evolve outside these announcements.
- Some of the yield changes following the announcements may be due to non-QE factors.

However, these communications may have changed expectations for QE, and including this broader set allows us to potentially capture those changes.

Our second strategy looks at the reaction of US interest rates to the Federal Open Market Committee's announcement of its first QE program following the 2008–09 global financial crisis. We take this second approach because this QE announcement was more unexpected and therefore has a better chance of measuring the full yield impact of a QE program. However, this is not an apples-to-apples comparison since the Federal Reserve's first QE program was implemented in response to a different kind of crisis (i.e., a banking crisis, not a pandemic) and purchased mortgage-backed securities in addition to US Treasuries.[7] Further, the impact of QE in a small open economy may be different from its impact in a large economy (Diez de los Rios and Shamloo 2017).

Our third strategy looks at three announcements in which the Bank of Canada reduced its QE program. Although these announcements were largely expected, we assume that each announcement got people to expect a $1 billion weekly increase in supply 13 weeks sooner than they otherwise would have started expecting it (the period of one *Monetary Policy Report* and interest rate decision cycle). A reduction in purchases of $13 billion per announcement resulted in a total reduction of $39 billion across the three announcements.[8] We then scale up to get a yield impact for the total program size of about $340 billion.

Event study analysis

We conduct an event study by analyzing the reactions of financial markets to Bank of Canada policy announcements on dates between March 2020 until October 2021. Our sample covers three distinct periods:

- **Pre-GBPP announcements**, covering two announcements when the Bank made interest rate cuts on March 3, 2020, and March 14, 2020.
- **GBPP-related announcements**, which include five announcements between March 27, 2020, and September 9, 2020.
- **Reduction-related announcements**, including nine announcements between October 28, 2020, and October 27, 2021.

We include pre-GBPP announcement dates because market participants may have already developed expectations for QE before March 27, 2020, due to the severity of the economic shock and the fact that interest rates were approaching their lower bound.[9] Analyzing reduction-related announcements allows us to assess the impact of a decrease in expectations for stimulus as economic conditions improved. We focus our analysis on announcements rather than operations, under the assumption that efficient financial markets should quickly incorporate the impact of the Bank's news into prices.[10]

We look at the changes in various financial asset prices from 10 minutes before to 20 minutes after an announcement is made. Using a narrow event-study window ensures that the asset prices are less likely to be influenced by any other significant (non-QE) macroeconomic events, thereby enhancing the accuracy of our estimation. For example, Prime Minister Trudeau made a speech announcing a large fiscal package on March 27, 2020, at 11:15 a.m., which was just a few hours after the Bank's GBPP announcement. The fiscal package announcement would have an impact on expected GoC bond supply and, consequently, bond yields. Furthermore, our methodology of using a narrow window is consistent with the literature analyzing the impact of central bank announcements on financial markets (Gürkaynak, Sack and Swanson 2005; Swanson 2017; Feunou et al. 2017).

To identify the impact of QE, we examine the changes in several financial instruments. The first financial asset we look at is the 90-day bankers' acceptance futures (BAX) contracts that trade on the Montréal Exchange. We use BAX to measure market participants' expectations of future short-term interest rates. Specifically, we calculate the change in the three-month Canadian BAX contract that expires between two and three quarters from the time of each individual announcement.[11] Using a similar method, we also calculate the changes in the yields of 2-year, 5-year and 10-year GoC benchmark bonds obtained from the Market Trade Reporting System 2.0,[12] the price of S&P TSX 60 standard futures that trade on the Montréal Exchange, and the USD/CAD exchange rate obtained from Refinitiv.

We start by examining the change in market prices around the Bank's two interest rate announcements in early March 2020 (we label these announcements "pre-GBPP"). Although these announcements preceded the Bank's initial GBPP announcement, market participants may have increased their expectations for QE when the Bank lowered its interest rate toward the effective lower bound. Further, the Bank stated in these announcements that it was ready to supply liquidity; this may also have increased market expectations for QE. These pre-GBPP announcements caused a reduction in bond and money market yields that was more pronounced at shorter maturities (**Table 1**, panel a). More specifically, the announcements on March 4, 2020, and March 13, 2020, led to decreases in BAX yields of approximately 18 bps.[13] Moreover, 2-year, 5-year and 10-year GoC bond yields declined around these announcements by 8 bps, 17 bps and 10 bps, respectively. The decline in shorter maturities was likely due to decreased expectations for short-term rates because of the interest rate portion of the announcements. However, some of the decline in the longer-maturity yields may have been due to increased expectations for QE.

Next, we analyze market movements around the five GBPP-related announcements. There is a cumulative decrease of about 15 bps, 11 bps and 11 bps in 2-year, 5-year and 10-year yields, respectively, in the window around these announcements. The most important of these announcements in terms of market reaction was the initial announcement of the GBPP on March 27, 2020. It resulted in a decrease of 9–14 bps on benchmark GoC bond yields (**Table 1**, panel b). The decline in bond yields around this announcement is consistent with the decline observed in Arora et al. (2021). The announcement of the GBPP lowered equity prices by about 55 bps but had a negligible impact on the value of the Canadian dollar against the US dollar. Only minor changes in financial market prices occurred across the other four announcements in the GBPP period. This is not surprising because the Bank did not change the GBPP program in any of these announcements.[14]

Table 1: Changes in yields and financial variables around key Bank of Canada announcement dates

Date	Bankers' acceptance futures	2-year yields	5-year yields	10-year yields	Equity	Foreign exchange
Panel A: Pre-GBPP						
March 4, 2020	-11.2	-10.6	-7.9	-5.3	21.9	-42.3
March 13, 2020	-7.0	2.9	-9.0	-4.7	285.7	-24.8
Total Pre-GBPP	**-18.2**	**-7.8**	**-16.9**	**-10.0**	**307.6**	**-67.1**
Panel B: GBPP						
March 27, 2020	-1.3	-14.2	-12.9	-8.5	-55.5	-3.4
April 15, 2020	0.0	-0.8	-1.0	-2.6	-1.0	3.2
June 3, 2020	2.3	0.7	2.2	2.3	-3.2	26.5
July 15, 2020	-0.5	-0.7	0.3	-1.9	19.2	-4.9
September 9, 2020	-0.5	0.3	0.3	0.0	-3.1	9.2
Total GBPP	**-0.1**	**-14.6**	**-11.1**	**-10.7**	**-43.5**	**30.6**
Panel C: Reduction						
October 28, 2020	-0.2	0.6	0.2	-0.2	-54.3	-24.4
December 9, 2020	0.1	0.1	0.6	0.9	-19.7	10.8
January 20, 2021	0.8	1.1	1.6	1.5	-10.8	48.1
March 10, 2021	-1.3	-1.3	-0.8	0.7	-12.9	-19.3
April 21, 2021	3.3	5.3	6.3	5.0	-25.9	91.1
June 9, 2021	0.5	0.0	0.6	0.0	-10.5	-8.3
July 14, 2021	-7.2	-3.2	-4.5	-3.4	33.4	-31.6
September 8, 2021	-0.5	-0.3	-1.1	0.0	4.0	-2.5
October 27, 2021	37.4	25.2	12.0	7.2	-48.3	76.0
Total Reduction	**32.9**	**27.6**	**14.9**	**11.6**	**-145.0**	**140.0**

Note: GBPP is Government of Canada Bond Purchase Program. We look at the changes in the prices of various financial assets from 10 minutes before to 20 minutes after an announcement is made. We use the implied rate of the three-quarter-ahead three-month bankers' acceptance futures, 2-, 5- and 10-year Government of Canada benchmark rates, log of the price of the S&P/TSX 60 index standard futures, and the USD/CAD exchange rate. The unit is in basis points.

Finally, we look at the market reaction to the Bank's nine announcements during the reduction period. The overall impact on prices throughout the reduction period is the reverse of the impact over pre-GBPP and GBPP-related sample periods (**Table 1**, panel c). This is intuitive—the Bank decreased its weekly QE purchases, and the announcements in this period likely reduced market expectations of the size of the QE program. The largest impact is observed on October 27, 2021, when the Bank announced the end of QE and entered the reinvestment phase. Following this announcement, the yield on BAX and GoC bonds increased. The increase was more pronounced for shorter maturities, reflecting an increase in expectations for short-term interest rates. Short-term rates increased by 37 bps, while long-term rates increased by 7 bps. The markets interpreted this announcement as signalling that the Bank would begin increasing interest rates sooner than the markets had previously thought, given that the Bank stated in its October 2021 *Monetary Policy Report* that economic slack would be absorbed by the middle quarters of 2022, earlier than its previous estimate of the second half of 2022.

Our event-study estimate of the impact of QE on financial markets depends on how narrowly we interpret announcements as being related to QE. If we look only at the GBPP period, GoC 10-year bond yields declined by a total of about 10 bps around the announcements. If we assume that the decline in 10-year yields around the announcements of March 4, 2020, and March 13, 2020, was due to increased expectations for QE, the estimated decline becomes larger, about 21 bps. On the one hand, our event-study analysis may underestimate the financial market impact of QE because it captures only how the announcements changed expectations for QE and not their full impact. On the other hand, it may overestimate the impact because it assumes that the decline in yields around the early-March announcements was due to QE and not due to the rate cuts themselves. On balance, we are likely still underestimating the impact on financial markets. The 12 bps increase in 10-year yields around the reduction announcements also suggests we may be underestimating QE.

To put our estimate of the impact of QE in Canada into perspective, **Chart 3** compares the impact of QE on 10-year government bond yields and the size of purchases across different countries and programs. The circles represent QE programs announced in response to the global financial crisis, and the triangles represent QE programs announced during the COVID-19 pandemic period. The chart shows no clear relationship between the size of the purchases and the impact on 10-year bond yields. The lack of a relationship between size and impact could be due to several factors, such as the size of the economy, how unexpected the announcements were or whether the country was at the zero lower bound when it announced QE. For example, Japan's QE was larger in size than that of other countries, but it likely had a small impact because it was announced when Japanese bond yields were already close to the effective lower bound. Unsurprisingly, the first large-asset purchase program (QE1) in the United States and the Asset Purchase Facility in the United Kingdom, the first QE program in each country, had the largest effects. The Bank of Canada's GBPP program is in the middle in terms of impact.

Chart 3: Estimates of the impact of quantitative easing on 10-year yields, by size of program

Size of asset purchase programs as a percentage of domestic GDP

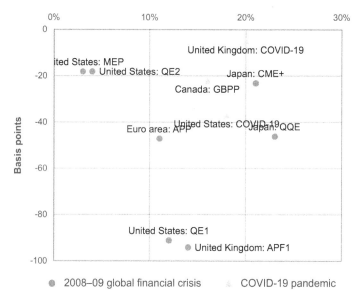

● 2008–09 global financial crisis   ● COVID-19 pandemic

Note: The horizontal axis measures the size of the purchases conducted within each program as a share of domestic GDP. The data during the global financial crisis period are based on the study by Andrade et al. (2016). APF1 stands for Asset Purchase Facility 1, APP stands for asset purchase programme, CME stands for Comprehensive Monetary Easing (where "+" denotes an extended period), MEP stands for maturity extension programme, and QQE stands for Quantitative and Qualitative Easing.

Impact on the macroeconomy

In this section, we estimate the effects of the QE announcements on the macroeconomy. Various approaches have been used to estimate the macroeconomic effects of QE in different economies. The Committee on the Global Financial System (CGFS 2019) conducts a review of 25 studies using mostly DSGE and VAR models. Overall, the effects are estimated as positive for both real output and inflation. Depending on the specific methodology adopted, the central bank and the program, the estimates of the peak response of real GDP and inflation show a lot of variation. The estimates for the effects of QE on GDP and inflation are both in the range of between 0 and 4 percentage points.

The details for the model used in this paper can be found in Zhang (2021), whose framework is based on the model of Gertler and Karadi (2011, 2013). Gertler and Karadi (2011, 2013) modify a reasonably standard New Keynesian model to explicitly include a banking sector and banking sector balance sheets. The model makes three primary assumptions to incorporate the role of QE:

- Banks finance risky, long-term assets with riskless, short-term debt.
- The existence of an agency problem between households and banks constrains the borrowing ability of the latter and generates excess returns between long- and short-term debts.
- The central bank conducts long-term asset purchases during economic crises and boosts the economy by reducing the credit costs of the banking sector.

Building on Gertler and Karadi (2011, 2013), Zhang (2021) adds the following three features to the model. All three are needed to study forward guidance and asset purchase policies in one framework and the effects of the policies on the entire yield curve.

- First, the paper introduces a nominal shadow overnight interest rate that follows a Taylor rule. The shadow overnight rate is the same as the observed overnight rate when the zero lower bound is not binding and is negative when the zero lower bound is binding.
- Second, the paper outlines a forward guidance shock, in the form of an announcement of future shocks to the Taylor rule, as a modelling device for generating innovations in expected future interest rates.
- Third, the paper presents a flexible approximation to interpolate the full yield curve using the shadow rate and the rate on a perpetuity.

In the model, forward guidance and asset purchases influence the yield curve differently:

- When at the zero lower bound, a central bank can announce an easing forward guidance policy to keep the overnight rate low in the near future. The forward guidance policy lowers expectations for future policy rates, thus decreasing short- to medium-term yields more than long-term yields. This forward guidance shock can also represent the signalling component of asset purchases, as markets infer information about the future path of policy rates from the QE announcement.
- Asset purchases of long-term bonds, in contrast, reduce the term premium and will decrease long-term yields more than short-term yields.

These policies will also have indirect impacts on the yield curve that need to be accounted for. Since these policies raise the market's expectations for output and inflation, there will be feedback from these policies onto shorter-term yields. For instance, the impact of a forward guidance shock on short- to medium-term rates may be reduced because the market will expect the economy to improve. Such improvement will temper expectations for the time of liftoff from the zero lower bound and the path for the overnight rate. And, given the direct and indirect effects of these policies on the yield curve, the model can infer how much of a given shock is related to forward guidance and how much is related to large-scale asset purchases.

We then combine the model with observed yield data. We estimate the model so that the changes in the yields that the structural model predicts from a linear combination of the two types of shocks will match the observed changes in 2-year, 5-year and 10-year yields around QE announcements. We provide the model with three different scenarios of yield changes. In the first scenario we look only at QE announcements on fixed interest rate announcement dates. In the second scenario we add the two pre-GBPP March announcements to the sample. Since the first two scenarios estimate only the surprise component of the impact, in the third scenario we do a back-of-the-envelope calculation to estimate the full impact of the program on yields.

For the third scenario, we consider the three reduction-related announcements in April, July and October 2021. There was a cumulative increase of about 8.8 bps of 10-year GoC yield around these announcements. We estimate the change in the market's expectations for our balance sheet by assuming that market participants advanced their expectations of a $1 billion weekly reduction by a quarter of a year each time. Market participants were largely expecting these announcements, so this assumption may be a generous estimate of how much the market's expectations for supply changed. This assumption implies a surprise of $1 billion a week for 13 weeks, for a total of $13 billion for each announcement, and a total of $39 billion over all three announcements. If we linearly scale the 8.8 bps 10-year yield impact for $39 billion up to $340 billion, it implies an impact of 77 bps for the full program. If we assume a smaller change in market expectations for the supply of bonds, it implies a larger impact for the full program. This estimate of 77 bps is roughly the same size as the estimated impact of QE1 in the United States. Their QE1 program was more of a surprise (since it was their first QE announcement), so the impact estimated by the event study is likely closer to the total impact of QE1.[15]

Then, given observed changes in 2-year, 5-year and 10-year yields around a central bank announcement, the model can disentangle how each component—large-scale asset purchases and forward guidance—will impact inflation and GDP. We then feed the total change in 2-year, 5-year and 10-year GoC bond yields in the first two scenarios into the model to estimate the sizes of the forward guidance and QE shocks and their impact on GDP and inflation. For the third scenario, we use only the 10-year GoC bond yield and attribute all the changes to large-scale asset purchases.

The dynamic effects of QE on real GDP and inflation for each of the three scenarios are shown in **Chart 4**. The figure provides the impulse response only for the large-scale asset purchase portion of each scenario and not for the forward guidance portion of the scenario. We ignore the forward guidance portion because we want to concentrate on the impact of QE only. Some of the QE announcements were accompanied by interest rate changes, which would be reflected in the impact of the forward guidance portion.

The peak impact of QE on real GDP, presented in **Chart 4**, panel a, occurs about three to four quarters after the shock and ranges from about 0.14% for scenario 1 to about 3% for scenario 3. Scenario 3, which is meant to capture both the expected and the surprise component of QE, is in the middle of the range CGFS (2019) provides for the estimated impact of QE on GDP in different countries. Similarly, **Chart 4**, panel b, shows that the peak impact for inflation is highest for scenario 3. The peak effect is around 1.8 percentage points. The inflationary impact of QE is in the lower end of the range of cross-country estimates provided in CGFS (2019), who find a range between 0 and 4 percentage points.

Chart 4: Dynamic effects of quantitative easing in three scenarios

a. Impulse response of real GDP to QE

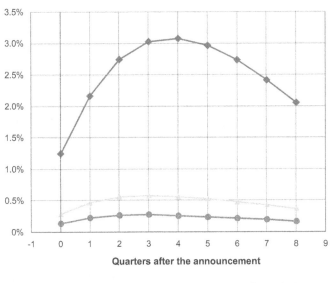

b. Impulse response of inflation to QE

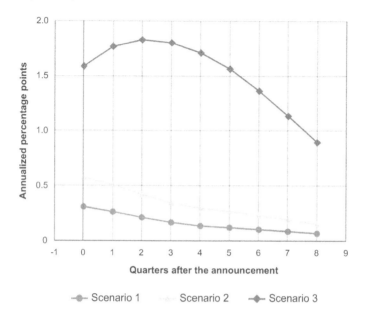

Conclusion

We provide an overview of the Bank's GBPP and discuss the theories for how QE transmits to financial markets and the macroeconomy. We also discuss the challenges inherent in estimating QE's impact. As a result of these challenges, the overall impact of QE is uncertain.

In this paper, we find that 10-year GoC bond yields decline by 10–20 bps around GBPP announcements. However, this change represents only the unexpected component of the total effect of QE, given that markets likely have expectations for QE before the announcements are made. While the counterfactual cannot be observed, and thus the impact of QE cannot be directly measured, the total effect of QE is likely much larger. In one scenario using back-of-the-envelope calculations, we estimate that the full QE effect is closer to 80 bps on the 10-year yield. We consider a range of scenarios to estimate the macroeconomic impact. We use a model that maps yield impacts into impacts on GDP and inflation to estimate the effect of QE on these two variables. In a scenario that considers the full impact of QE, the model suggests QE has a peak impact of about 3% on GDP and 1.8% on inflation.

There is considerable uncertainty around the impact of QE on bond yields, and likely more uncertainty about the impact of QE on GDP and inflation. Therefore, these estimates should be taken with a grain of salt. Moreover, models of QE do not capture the potential for QE to eliminate negative tail outcomes. For example, in the counterfactual model of the absence of QE, it is possible there could have been a much larger increase in yields than we consider in our 80 bps scenario because the market would have to absorb an extra $340 billion of issuance. And the model does not capture the possibility that QE helps avoid a large, negative macroeconomic outcome.

Several questions remain unexplored:

- The demand for government bonds could be nonlinear, and this nonlinearity is not directly observed. We assess the reactions of financial markets around the time of QE announcements; however, a great deal of uncertainty remains about the shape of the demand curve. This is because these announcements do not provide much information about the impact of large changes in government debt outstanding and, hence, the overall impact of QE.
- While we know that the impact of QE (and QT) depends on the institutional and economic environment, we do not have good estimates of how much different factors matter.
- Our estimate of the macroeconomic impacts of QE is based on a closed-economy macroeconomic model. The transmission of QE may be different in small open economies such as Canada.

We leave these questions to future research.

References

Andrade, P., J. Breckenfelder, F. De Fiore, P. Karadi and O. Tristani. 2016. "The ECB's Asset Purchase Programme: An Early Assessment." European Central Bank Discussion Paper No. 1956.

Arora, R., S. Gungor, J. Nesrallah, G. Ouellet Leblanc and J. Witmer. 2021. **"The Impact of the Bank of Canada's Government Bond Purchase Program."** Bank of Canada Staff Analytical Note No. 2021-23.

Bank of Canada. 2015. **"Framework for Conducting Monetary Policy at Low Interest Rates."** December.

Bank of Canada. 2020. **"Bank of Canada maintains target for the overnight rate, scales back some market operations as financial conditions improve."** Press release, June 3.

Bauer, M. and G. Rudebusch. 2014. "The Signaling Channel for Federal Reserve Bond Purchases." *International Journal of Central Banking* 10 (3): 233-289.

Chen, H., V. Cúrdia and A. Ferrero. 2012. "The Macroeconomic Effects of Large-Scale Asset Purchase Programmes." *Economic Journal* 122 (564): F289–F315.

Christensen, J. H. and J. M. Gillan. 2022. "Does Quantitative Easing Affect Market Liquidity?" *Journal of Banking and Finance* 134: 106349.

Chu P., G. Johnson, S. Kinnear, K. McGuinness and M. McNeely. 2022. "**Settlement Balances Deconstructed**." Bank of Canada Staff Analytical Note No. 2022-13.

Committee on the Global Financial System. 2019. "Unconventional Monetary Policy Tools: A Cross-Country Analysis." Bank for International Settlements CGFS Paper No. 63.

Diez de los Rios, A. and M. Shamloo. 2017. "Quantitative Easing and Long-Term Yields in Small Open Economies." International Monetary Fund Working Paper No. 17/212.

Du, W., K. Forbes and M. Luzzetti. 2024. "Quantitative Tightening Around the Globe: What Have We Learned?" National Bureau of Economic Research Working Paper No. 32321.

Duffie, D. and F. Keane. 2023. "Market-Function Asset Purchases." Federal Reserve Bank of New York Staff Report No. 1054.

Feunou, B., C. Garriott, J. Kyeong and R. Leiderman. 2017. "**The Impacts of Monetary Policy Statements**." Bank of Canada Staff Analytical Note No. 2017-22.

Fontaine, J.-S., H. Ford and A. Walton. 2020. "**COVID-19 and Bond Market Liquidity: Alert, Isolation and Recovery**." Bank of Canada Staff Analytical Note No. 2020-14.

Gertler, M. and P. Karadi. 2011. "A Model of Unconventional Monetary Policy." *Journal of Monetary Economics* 58 (1): 17–34.

Gertler, M. and P. Karadi. 2013. "QE 1 vs. 2 vs. 3: A Framework for Analyzing Large Scale Asset Purchases as a Monetary Policy Tool." *International Journal of Central Banking* 9 (1): 5–53.

Gürkaynak, R. S., B. Sack and E. T. Swanson. 2005. "Do Actions Speak Louder than Words? The Response of Asset Prices to Monetary Policy Actions and Statements." *International Journal of Central Banking* 1 (1): 55–93.

Johnson, G. 2023. "**A Review of the Bank of Canada's Market Operations Related to COVID-19**." Bank of Canada Staff Discussion Paper No. 2023-6.

Kabaca, S. 2016. "**Quantitative Easing in a Small Open Economy: An International Portfolio Balancing Approach**." Bank of Canada Staff Working Paper No. 2016-55.

King, T. 2019. "Expectation and Duration at the Effective Lower Bound." *Journal of Financial Economics* 134 (3): 736–760.

Krishnamurthy, A. and A. Vissing-Jorgensen. 2011. "The Effects of Quantitative Easing on Interest Rates: Channels and Implications for Policy." National Bureau of Economic Research Working Paper No. 17555.

Krishnamurthy, A. and A. Vissing-Jorgensen. 2012. "The Aggregate Demand for Treasury Debt." *Journal of Political Economy* 120 (2): 233–267.

Neely, C. 2015. "Unconventional Monetary Policy Had Large International Effects." *Journal of Banking and Finance* 52: 101–111.

S. Poloz. 2020a. **"Press Conference Opening Statement."** Ottawa, Ontario, March 27.

S. Poloz. 2020b. **"Opening Statement before the House of Commons Standing Committee on Finance."** Ottawa, Ontario, April 16.

Sutherland, C. S. 2023. "Forward Guidance and Expectation Formation: A Narrative Approach." *Journal of Applied Econometrics* 38 (2): 222–241.

Swanson, E. T. 2017. "Measuring the Effects of Federal Reserve Forward Guidance and Asset Purchases on Financial Markets." National Bureau of Economic Research Working Paper No. 23311.

Vayanos, D. and J.-L. Vila. 2021. "A Preferred-Habitat Model of the Term Structure of Interest Rates. *Econometrica* 89 (1): 77–112.

Vieira, P. 2024. **"Bank Of Canada Is Sticking With Its Quantitative Tightening Plan."** *Wall Street Journal*, March 21.

Vissing-Jorgensen, A. 2021. "The Treasury Market in Spring 2020 and the Response of the Federal Reserve." *Journal of Monetary Economics* 124: 19–47.

Wallace, N. 1981. "A Modigliani-Miller Theorem for Open-Market Operations." *American Economic Review* 71 (3): 267–274.

Weale, M. and T. Wieladek. 2022. "Financial Effects of QE and Conventional Monetary Policy Compared." *Journal of International Money and Finance* 127: 102673.

Zhang, X. 2021. **"Evaluating the Effects of Forward Guidance and Large-Scale Asset Purchases."** Bank of Canada Staff Working Paper No. 2021-54.

Endnotes

1. We use the terms GBPP and QE interchangeably in this note. The Bank introduced several other asset purchase programs for provincial government and non-government securities, but these programs are not discussed in this paper.[←]

2. For more on the Bank's policy actions in response to the COVID-19 pandemic, see Poloz 2020b.[←]

3. For more on settlement balances, see Chu et al. (2022).[←]

4. A 25 bps decrease in 10-year yields provides more stimulus than a 25 bps decrease in the overnight rate since the overnight rate cut likely will not persist for 10 years. From January 2008 through July 2023, there have been 11 interest rate announcements where the short-term rate (as proxied by the first bankers' acceptance futures contract) moved by more than 10 bps after the announcement. On average across these announcements, the short-term rate moved by about 19 bps, whereas 10-year yields moved by only 6 bps (both in absolute value terms).[←]

5. See also P. Beaudry, "**Our quantitative easing operations: Looking under the hood**," Remarks delivered virtually to the Greater Moncton Chamber of Commerce, the Fredericton Chamber of Commerce and the Saint John Region Chamber of Commerce December 10, 2020.[←]

6. The QE neutrality result also assumes that QE has no impact on fiscal policy.[←]

7. The share of QE that was expected before it was announced may have been larger during the pandemic since expectations for government debt expansion (e.g., shifts of the vertical line S_B in **Figure 2** to the right) would have been larger in both Canada and the United States during the pandemic than during the global financial crisis.[←]

8. To keep the analysis simple, we assume that these announcements do not contain any information that would lead to potential shifts in expectations of the maturity structure of the Bank's purchases.[←]

9. The disfunction observed in the GoC bond market (Fontaine, Ford and Walton 2020) may have also contributed to increased expectations for QE.[←]

10. In addition to looking at changes around the Bank's interest rate decision dates, we also measure the changes in prices of financial assets on the Bank's auction announcement dates, auction operation dates and dates when Governing Council members made speeches (not shown). The changes in market prices that happened around all these announcement dates were small.[←]

11. Three-month Canadian BAX contracts represent some of the most liquid and heavily traded instruments in the Canadian money market. In particular, BAX reflect the three-month Canadian Dollar Offered Rate (CDOR), expressed as an interest rate per annum. Three years of quarterly BAX contracts are listed at all times. The standard quarterly cycle consists of March, June, September and December. For example, on the April 15, 2020, interest announcement date, we use the contract that expires in December 2020; the rate reflected in the contract can be interpreted as market participants' expectations for the three-month CDOR on the last trading day in December 2020.[←]

12. The estimated impact does not change much if we measure it using prices of 2-, 5- and 10-year GoC bond futures, traded on the Montréal Exchange, to calculate the implied yield changes.[←]

13. To support the functioning of the bankers' acceptance market, the Bank announced its intention to launch the Bankers' Acceptance Purchase Facility (BAPF) around 2:00 p.m. on March 13, 2020. This coincides with the event window used for the March 13, 2020, announcement (2:08 p.m.) The observed decline in BAX yields around the March 13 announcement could be contaminated by the impact of the BAPF announcement. However, given that the BAX we look at expire in three to four quarters and that short-term bond yields declined by a similar amount, it seems likely that most of the change in the yield of the BAX contract was due to the Bank's interest rate announcement.[←]

14. All the financial assets we examined following the Bank's June 3, 2020, announcement experienced small changes. On that date, the Bank announced a reduction in the frequency of its term repurchase agreement (repo) operations and its purchases of bankers' acceptances due to improved financial conditions. Specifically, we observe an increase in the yields of BAX, GoC bonds and the USD/CAD exchange rate, and a decrease in the yield of equity futures.[←]

15. On March 21, 2024, Deputy Governor Gravelle reiterated the Bank's view that the steady-state level of settlement balances was in a range of $20 billion to $60 billion. Meanwhile, some participants had estimated that the steady state settlement balances would be higher, with one market participant suggesting around $80 billion (Vieira 2024). Ten-year yields increased by about 4 bps in the window around this speech. If we assume that the impact of QT is as large as the impact of QE and that the speech changed the market's expectations for QT by $15 billion to $25 billion, we can generate another estimate of the impact of QE by scaling that impact up to the full QE amount of $340 billion. Overall, the market reaction would suggest a 10-year yield impact of 54–90 bps when we scale to the full QE amount. However, this may be an underestimate since the announcement effects of QT have tended to be smaller than the announcement effects of QE (Du, Forbes and Luzzetti 2024).[↩]

Disclaimer

Bank of Canada staff discussion papers are completed staff research studies on a wide variety of subjects relevant to central bank policy, produced independently from the Bank's Governing Council. This research may support or challenge prevailing policy orthodoxy. Therefore, the views expressed in this paper are solely those of the authors and may differ from official Bank of Canada views. No responsibility for them should be attributed to the Bank.

Content Type(s): **Staff research, Staff discussion papers**
Research Topic(s): **Financial institutions, Financial markets, Financial system regulation and policies, Inflation and prices, Monetary policy, Monetary policy transmission**
JEL Code(s): **E, E5, E52, E58, G, G2, G21, G28**
DOI: https://doi.org/10.34989/sdp-2024-5

Reprinted with the permission of the Bank of Canada, 2025.

Could all-to-all trading improve liquidity in the Government of Canada bond market?

Staff Analytical Note 2024-17 (English)
Jabir Sandhu, Rishi Vala
July 2024

Introduction

Government bond markets are typically considered to be among the most-liquid fixed-income markets. Even so, liquidity conditions in government bond markets can deteriorate sharply when a sudden imbalance occurs between the demand for and supply of liquidity. In fact, in recent extreme episodes of market turmoil like the onset of the COVID-19 crisis in March 2020 and the UK gilt crisis in September 2022, market liquidity deteriorated so much that central banks intervened by buying government bonds to stabilize and restore orderly functioning of these markets.

Some policy-makers, academics and financial market participants believe that one reason market liquidity of government bonds is vulnerable to periods of market turmoil is because the structure of these markets is centred around dealers. In this type of market structure, dealers use their own balance sheets or act as a broker to match offsetting transactions between their different clients. In periods of turmoil, however, client demands for liquidity can surge, and trading can become more one-sided. In other words, many clients trade bonds in the same direction, by, for example, buying government bonds in a flight to safety or selling government bonds in a dash for cash.

Dealers may charge a higher fee to intermediate such trades as compensation for the additional risks that they bear on their own balance sheets when market conditions are volatile.[1] In extreme cases, dealers may stop intermediating completely, either due to constraints on their balance sheets or their inability to hedge risks. This could prevent transactions from occurring among clients who would otherwise be willing to transact with one another.

Adopting an all-to-all market structure is one of several proposals for improving the resilience of government bond markets during periods of turmoil (Duffie 2023). In this structure, market participants would be able to transact directly with each other on an electronic trading platform and therefore avoid any limits in dealers' ability to intermediate. An all-to-all structure could also attract new market participants through increased transparency of executable and executed prices on all-to-all trading platforms. This increased transparency could improve the bargaining power of market participants and reduce barriers to entry that may exist in a dealer-intermediated structure. Supporters of all-to-all trading argue that a more diverse set of market participants could improve market liquidity. This is because it could increase the likelihood and amount of bond transactions occurring in opposite directions, even during periods of turmoil. These offsetting transactions could reduce pressures on market liquidity.

To examine these considerations of all-to-all trading, we use granular transaction-level data to assess how much client-to-client trading could be possible in the Government of Canada (GoC) bond market. We find, on average, almost half of the GoC bond transactions of dealers' clients could potentially be offset with those of other clients over the trading day. This share is stable over time, including during the COVID-19 crisis in March 2020. This demonstrates that clients were indeed transacting in the opposite direction of other clients' transactions in a period of market turmoil. For GoC bond futures—instruments that are like GoC bonds but trade on an all-to-all platform—we find that almost all clients' transactions can be offset by those of other clients and that this high offsetting share is also stable.

So would all-to-all trading support liquidity in the GoC bond market? The answer remains unclear. On the one hand, our results shed some light on the potential for clients' transactions to offset each other. On the other hand, our methodology overlooks important considerations for the sake of simplicity. For instance, we do not account for differences in the prices when offsetting client transactions or for the influence that client-dealer relationships may have on trading behaviours. These considerations make it challenging to understand whether our estimated extent of client offsetting would take place if GoC bonds were traded entirely on an all-to-all platform. In addition, several other aspects of all-to-all trading merit further investigation.

All-to-all trading presents a range of risks and considerations

While all-to-all trading may bring benefits, it presents a range of risks and considerations. Critics argue that the potential for matching transactions across different participants could be minimal in periods of market turmoil. They argue that even new entrants could have demands for liquidity that lead them to transact government bonds in the same direction as other clients, amplifying one-sided trading rather than promoting matching. Some critics also argue that new entrants and existing clients would have fewer incentives to maintain intermediation services in periods of turmoil. They cite the lower importance on relationships with clients on an all-to-all platform compared with a dealer-intermediated structure as the reason for the potential reduction in intermediation services.

Other considerations that require further analysis include:

- the impact of greater price transparency on an all-to-all platform can affect the behaviour of market participants
- the impacts to settlement and clearing risks as clients' transactions are executed on an all-to-all platform
- the potential negative impacts to other services provided by dealers, such as access to primary bond markets
- the implications for markets, such as repurchase (repo) or derivatives markets, that trade in conjunction with GoC bonds
- the potential reduction of capital that dealers allocate to their intermediation businesses

Almost half of transactions could potentially be offset on any given trading day

Using data from October 2019 to November 2023 on GoC bond transactions from the Market Trade Reporting System, we calculate the share of transactions of clients of dealers that could have potentially been offset by transactions with other clients within a trading day, following Chaboud et al. (2022).[2] In other words, for each purchase of a specific bond that a client makes, what share of the amount bought was sold by other clients on the same trading day and vice versa. The methodology allows buys and sells to offset each other despite potential differences in the prices of trades or the exact times within the day that trade trades occurred.[3] It also does not match exact trade amounts; instead, it looks at total buys and sells for a specific bond. Despite these limitations, our methodology helps establish estimates of how many client transactions in a trading day could potentially be matched.

Chart 1 reports the average daily amount of GoC bond transactions that can be offset by clients as a share of the amount of transactions offset plus the residual amount that is not offset. Across all types of GoC bonds, 49% of client transactions could be offset on an average trading day. Across bond tenors, the offsetting shares range from 57% to 65% for benchmark bonds and from 23% to 46% for non-benchmark bonds.

The higher offsetting shares for benchmark bonds is likely due to their greater liquidity, which leads to higher turnover of trading volume compared with that of non-benchmark bonds (Gungor and Yang 2017). The relatively lower offsetting share for non-benchmark bonds suggests that dealers play an important role in using their balance sheets to intermediate these less-liquid bonds. Overall, high offsetting transactions among clients promote two-sided markets. This can help dealers more easily find the bonds or cash they need to fulfill their clients' transactions, which could promote market liquidity (Sandhu and Vala 2023a).

Chart 1: Benchmark bonds have higher average daily shares of offsetting client transactions than those of non-benchmark bonds

Daily average, 25th and 75th percentile centred around averages

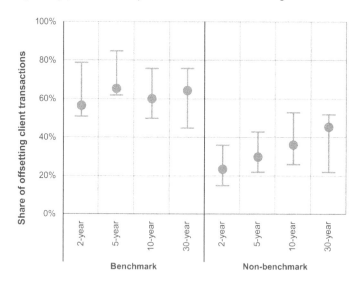

Sources: Market Trade Reporting System and Bank of Canada calculations
Last observation: November 24, 2023

The share of offsetting transactions was stable during the COVID-19 crisis

In this section, we examine how the share of clients' offsetting GoC bond transactions changes over time, including in periods of market turmoil. Client-to-client trading could be most beneficial in periods of market turmoil when a larger share of clients, like asset managers, may experience an increased need for liquidity. This type of client-to-client trading would also reduce the volume of transactions that dealers would need to intermediate using their own balance sheets, which they may be more reluctant to do in periods of turmoil.

Chart 2 shows the 21-day moving average of the total daily share of clients' offsetting GoC bond transactions with the offsetting and residual amounts. The share of clients' offsetting transactions is fairly stable, at around 50%, from October 2019 to November 2023. The offsetting share was also stable during the COVID-19 crisis in March 2020, indicating that many clients were transacting GoC bonds in the opposite direction despite significant market turmoil.

Chart 2: The share of offsetting client transactions was stable during the COVID-19 crisis

21-day moving average, daily data

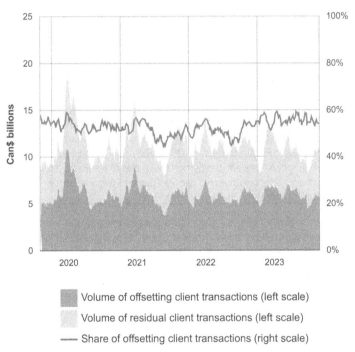

■ Volume of offsetting client transactions (left scale)
■ Volume of residual client transactions (left scale)
— Share of offsetting client transactions (right scale)

Sources: Market Trade Reporting System and Bank of Canada calculations
Last observation: November 24, 2023

While our analysis sheds light on the share of client transactions that could potentially be offset, our estimates of clients' offsetting transactions could have been different if clients had actually traded on an all-to-all platform. This difference arises because our estimates are based on trading behaviour that is influenced by the relationships between dealers and their clients. These relationships are typically formed in dealer-intermediated market structures, like the repo market for GoC treasury bills (Sandhu, Walton and Lee 2019). For instance, dealers can encourage their clients to conduct a trade that they otherwise may not have entered. They could do this by offering price concessions or packaging a GoC bond with other services or products offered to their clients.

As a result, our estimates may be higher than what we would observe on an all-to-all platform given the influence of relationships between dealers and their clients.

Almost all bond futures transactions could potentially offset each other

To understand what client-to-client trading could look like without the influence of dealer-to-client relationships on trading behaviour, we apply our methodology to the GoC bond futures market. In other words, we calculate the share of client transactions that could be offset by other clients for each bond futures contract each day, ignoring individual transaction amounts and any difference in prices or time of the trade over the course of the trading day.[4] Like our analysis of GoC bonds, this exercise is useful for understanding whether trading among clients is two-sided at the daily level for GoC bond futures.

GoC bond futures can be a substitute for GoC bonds because they offer similar exposure to interest rates. GoC bond futures, however, are transacted entirely on a futures exchange, which is akin to an all-to-all platform, where clients can trade directly with other clients or dealers anonymously. In this market structure, relationships between dealers and clients are less likely to form because dealers do not directly benefit from their clients' transactions.

Our comparison is imperfect due to several differences between GoC bonds and bond futures. These differences include the set of clients and dealers, standards for settling transactions and the amount of cash required to enter into positions. As well, futures trades are much smaller than those in the GoC bond market. Moreover, trading is more concentrated in bond futures because there are fewer active bond futures than there are different GoC bonds, possibly increasing their liquidity.

Chart 3 presents the 21-day moving average of the total daily share of offsetting client transactions in the GoC bond futures market as well as the offsetting and residual amounts. The offsetting share is quite stable over our entire sample, from January 2020 to June 2023, and transactions among clients that could potentially offset each other is high, at around 90% on average. In other words, approved participants—who are comparable to dealers in the GoC bond market—are on the other side of only 10% of client transactions over the trading day. These results demonstrate that a large amount of client-to-client trading indeed takes place on an all-to-all platform for an asset class that is like GoC bonds and is less influenced by the relationship between dealers and clients.

Chart 3: The share of offsetting client transactions in Government of Canada bond futures was stable during the COVID-19 crisis

21-day moving average, daily data

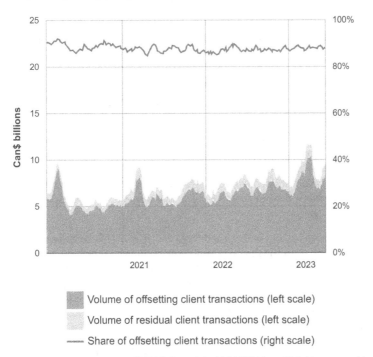

Sources: Montréal Exchange (TSX © Copyright 2024 TSX Inc. All rights reserved.) and Bank of Canada calculations
Last observation: June 9, 2023

Conclusion

We find that almost half of the GoC bond transactions from clients could be potentially offset by the transactions of other clients over the trading day. This share remains stable in periods of market turmoil. These results help address concerns with all-to-all trading around the potential for overwhelmingly one-sided transactions from clients in periods of turmoil. In the GoC bond futures market, we find that almost all of client transactions are ultimately offset by transactions of other clients. This demonstrates that clients are willing to trade a security similar to a GoC bond but traded on an all-to-all platform. Our results are an important first step in understanding the relevance of broader all-to-all trading in the GoC bond market. However, it remains unclear whether broader all-to-all trading would improve liquidity given the simplicity of our methodology as well as several other risks and considerations that merit further investigation.

Appendix: Robustness of clients' offsetting transactions

To ensure the approach of measuring clients' offsetting transactions used in our analysis is robust, we consider alternative methods and find that our overall conclusions hold. One caveat, however, is that we do not account for differences in the prices of buy and sell transactions in our offsetting methodology. Despite the robustness exercises discussed below, ignoring price differences overstates our offsetting potential results.

We calculate the same measure, but instead of offsetting buy and sell transactions for individual GoC bonds, we offset transactions according to broader categories based on the term to maturity of bonds. Specifically, we allow buys and sells of different bonds to offset each other if their term to maturity is between 1 and 3 years; between 3 and 8 years; between 8 and 12 years; and greater than 12 years.

Matching transactions within these broader buckets is plausible because bonds of similar maturity are close substitutes. Clients trading on an all-to-all platform may adjust their behaviour to trade substitutable bonds because the platform may foster greater price transparency and lower costs to locate available bonds for trade. Under this approach, the average daily clients' offsetting transaction for non-benchmark bonds, across all term-to-maturity buckets, increases by between 14 and 16 percentage points, depending on the term-to-maturity bucket.

For our analysis, we allow buy and sell transactions to offset at the daily level. This is a useful theoretical exercise to help understand whether client trading is one-sided during the day. In reality, clients may not be willing to be exposed to the risks of holding or being short a GoC bond or GoC bond future over the course of the trading day and may want to offset their trades immediately.

To understand the extent of client two-sided trading at shorter intervals, we apply our same offsetting approach, but at 1-hour and 15-minute intervals. For GoC bonds, this approach is only a rough approximation because the time stamps in the Market Trade Reporting System may be inaccurate. As expected, the share of clients' offsetting transactions declines at shorter intervals.[5] Despite these lower levels of client offsetting, the results remain indicative of two-sided trading among clients at shorter intervals, albeit to a lesser extent.

References

Chaboud, A., E. Correia Golay, C. Cox, M. Fleming, Y. Huh, F. Keane, K. Lee, K. Schwarz, C. Vega and C. Windover. 2022. "**All-to-All Trading in the U.S. Treasury Market.**" Federal Reserve Bank of New York Staff Report No. 1036.

Duffie, D. 2023. "**Resilience Redux in the US Treasury Market.**" Stanford University Graduate School of Business Research Paper No. 4552735. Presented at the Jackson Hole Symposium, Federal Reserve Bank of Kansas City.

Gungor, S. and J. Yang. 2017. "**Has Liquidity in Canadian Government Bond Markets Deteriorated?**" Bank of Canada Staff Analytical Note No. 2017-10.

Sandhu, J. and R. Vala. 2023a. "**Do Hedge Funds Support Liquidity in the Government of Canada Bond Market?**" Bank of Canada Staff Analytical Note No. 2023-11.

Sandhu, J. and R. Vala. 2023b. "**The Government of Canada Bond Market: Discussion on Market Structure.**" Presentation to the Canadian Fixed-Income Forum, Ottawa, Ontario, November 21.

Sandhu, J., A. Walton and J. Lee. 2019. "**Borrowing Costs for Government of Canada Treasury Bills.**" Bank of Canada Staff Analytical Note No. 2019-28.

Acknowledgements

We thank David Cimon, Jean-Philippe Dion, Toni Gravelle, Stéphane Lavoie and Adrian Walton for their comments. We are grateful to Harri Vikstedt and Corey Garriott for their advice and suggestions and to members of the Canadian Fixed-Income Forum for sharing their perspectives at their meeting in November 2023. We also thank Alain Chaboud, Ellen Correia Golay, Michael Fleming and Frank Keane for helpful discussions comparing our analysis to their work on all-to-all trading in the US Treasury Market. Finally, we are grateful to Robert Tasca and members of his team at the Montréal Exchange for providing data for our analysis.

Endnotes

1. Some market participants contend that measures of liquidity should be evaluated on a volatility-adjusted basis. When adjusted for volatility, some recent periods of worsened liquidity appear less severe.[←]

2. See Sandhu and Vala (2023a) for a description of the Market Trade Reporting System. [←]

3. Differences in prices of buy and sell transactions could be an important deterrent for clients to trade with each other. If price differences were considered, the potential for offsetting could be even lower when prices are volatile.[←]

4. We exclude 30-year GoC bond futures contracts from our analysis given the limited trading activity in this tenor.[←]

5. See Sandhu and Vala (2023b) for details of how clients' offsetting changes at shorter intervals.[←]

Disclaimer

Bank of Canada staff analytical notes are short articles that focus on topical issues relevant to the current economic and financial context, produced independently from the Bank's Governing Council. This work may support or challenge prevailing policy orthodoxy. Therefore, the views expressed in this note are solely those of the authors and may differ from official Bank of Canada views. No responsibility for them should be attributed to the Bank.

Content Type(s): **Staff research, Staff analytical notes**
Research Topic(s): **Coronavirus disease (COVID-19), Financial institutions, Financial markets, Financial stability, Market structure and pricing**
JEL Code(s): D, D4, D47, D5, D53, G, G0, G01, G1, G12, G13, G14, G2, G21, G23
DOI: https://doi.org/10.34989/san-2024-17

Reprinted with the permission of the Bank of Canada, 2025.

How foreign central banks can affect liquidity in the Government of Canada bond market

Staff Analytical Note 2024-26 (English)
Patrick Aldridge, Jabir Sandhu, Sofia Tchamova
December 2024

Introduction

Imagine it's Friday night and you're out for dinner at a busy restaurant with some friends. After an hour, you've all finished eating but decide to stay at your table for a bit longer to continue catching up.

Remaining at your table for longer presents a trade-off. Of course, you and your friends are allowed to stay at your table after your meal. In fact, you may even order drinks or desserts, generating more revenue for the restaurant. But staying reduces the number of tables available for other customers. This can lead to lengthier wait times or some guests potentially being turned away.

In a sense, financial assets are like tables at a restaurant. When investors hold their assets for long periods—often referred to as buy-and-hold investors—fewer of these assets are available for other investors. This can potentially worsen liquidity in secondary markets.

We examine the trading behaviour of foreign central banks and its potential impact on liquidity in the Government of Canada (GoC) bond market.[1] Our analysis builds on recent projects from staff at the Bank of Canada aimed at better understanding how asset managers can affect liquidity in Canadian fixed-income markets (**Sandhu and Vala 2023**; **Bédard-Pagé et al. 2021**). The Bank monitors liquidity in secondary markets and has different tools to support liquidity in certain circumstances. This is because liquid and well-functioning fixed-income markets are important for the transmission of monetary policy and the stability of the financial system.

We estimate that foreign central banks own at least 12% to 21% of the float of GoC bonds, which is the amount of GoC bonds outstanding minus the Bank's holdings. Foreign central banks also tend to hold their GoC bonds for longer than other market participants do.

This buy-and-hold behaviour can promote market stability because foreign central banks' trading decisions may be less sensitive to market conditions than those of other types of asset managers. In fact, during the peak period of market illiquidity in March 2020, foreign central banks had negligible trading flows, while many other types of asset managers sold GoC bonds, contributing to liquidity strains (**Sandhu and Vala 2023**).

In contrast, buy-and-hold behaviour could reduce the availability of GoC bonds in secondary markets, potentially reducing liquidity. We find that foreign central banks lend out only a small share of their bonds in the repo market—another sign of buy-and-hold behaviour. We also find that higher levels of foreign central bank holdings of GoC bonds are related to illiquidity. This is because their holdings have a positive and statistically significant relationship with borrowing volumes from primary dealers in the Bank's Securities Repo Operation (SRO), a program designed to support liquidity in securities-financing markets.

While our results show that foreign central banks' behaviour could promote illiquidity, that is only one part of the picture. Foreign central banks' participation in the GoC bond market offers many benefits beyond promoting stability in periods of turmoil. For example, their steady demand for GoC bonds can reduce the cost of funding for the federal government (**Lane 2019**; **Pomorski, Rivadeneyra and Wolfe 2014**).[2]

Central banks manage portfolios of foreign exchange reserves

Central banks—and, to a lesser extent, other authorities like governments—are portfolio managers for foreign exchange reserves. Foreign exchange reserves are assets held in currencies other than a country's domestic currency. These reserves allow central banks to intervene in their currency markets, potentially helping:

- promote a country's exports
- reduce capital outflows
- manage market volatility

Reserves can also provide a source of liquidity that can be leveraged to meet international financial obligations or to provide foreign currency to domestic institutions, among other reasons.

Given that reserves are held for precautionary purposes, central banks and governments typically manage reserve portfolios with the objectives of preserving capital and maintaining liquidity. Generating returns is a common tertiary objective conditional on meeting the first two goals. As a result, foreign exchange reserves are typically invested in securities that are highly liquid and of high credit quality, like highly rated government bonds and bills as well as securities issued by government agencies or sub-sovereign levels of governments (**Pomorski, Rivadeneyra and Wolfe 2014**).

Globally, foreign exchange reserves that are held or denominated in Canadian dollars have increased in recent years and are 2.39% of total reserve assets, which is small relative to currencies like the US dollar or euro (International Monetary Fund 2024). However, this share can be meaningful given that Canadian financial markets are smaller than markets in some other jurisdictions.

Foreign central banks are large players in the Government of Canada bond market

We learn about foreign central banks' presence in the market by examining their holdings of GoC bonds. Given the lack of a comprehensive dataset of foreign central banks' holdings, we estimate their holdings of GoC bonds by applying three approaches and using two different datasets. Together, the different approaches give us an idea of the possible levels of foreign central banks' holdings.

- First, we use data on the holdings of foreign central banks that have the Bank as their custodian. However, these data exclude foreign central banks that have other custodians for their Canadian investments.
- Second, we use data from the Market Trade Reporting System (MTRS) to accumulate the buy and sell transactions of GoC bonds in secondary markets where foreign central banks were counterparties and remove bonds that have matured to approximate their holdings (see **Sandhu and Vala 2023** for a description of these data). These data include a larger set of foreign central banks. However, the accumulation starts only in October 2019, so we exclude any bonds purchased and held before then from the approximation. Additionally, we do not capture transactions in the primary market or those with dealers that are not required to report their transactions to MTRS.
- Third, we consider the second approach using MTRS but include the initial holdings as at October 2019 for those central banks that use the Bank as their custodian.

Chart 1 shows the range of estimated holdings of foreign central banks using our three approaches. The holdings of foreign central banks could be at least 12% to 21% of the GoC bond float, showing that foreign central banks own a significant share of GoC bonds, regardless of the estimation approach.[3]

However, these estimates could understate the holdings of foreign central banks. Even when we combine the two datasets, we miss the initial holdings of those foreign central banks that use custodians other than the Bank of Canada.

Chart 1: Foreign central banks hold a significant share of the float of Government of Canada bonds

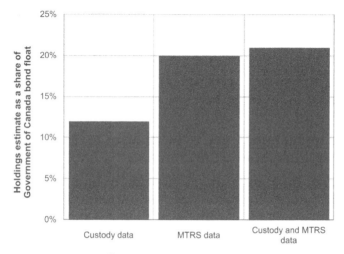

Data source used in estimation approach

Note: MTRS is Market Trade Reporting System. *Custody data* include holdings of foreign central banks that use the Bank of Canada as their custodian.
Sources: MTRS and Bank of Canada calculations
Last observation: June 10, 2024

Foreign central banks have long holding periods

Buy-and-hold behaviour presents a trade-off for liquidity conditions:

- On the one hand, buy-and-hold investors can promote stability in markets during periods of turmoil, unlike other investors who may trade quickly in response to market movements and amplify market strains. For instance, Sandhu and Vala (2023) show how hedge funds and other clients of dealers sold GoC bonds during the peak of market turmoil in March 2020, adding to strains on market liquidity. However, we find that foreign central banks had negligible trading flows during that period.
- On the other hand, buy-and-hold investors may also reduce liquidity because they effectively reduce the amount of securities available for other market participants. The potential impacts for market liquidity from the trading behaviour of foreign central banks may be greater than other types of market participants given their large presence in the GoC bond market.

Using MTRS data, we calculate the period between the purchase of a bond by each foreign central bank and the date that same bond was sold or had matured. For this estimated holding period, we consider only bonds that were both bought and sold or had matured during our sample period. Some bonds may have been purchased before the start of our sample period or sold after its end. We exclude these transactions from our calculation. For each foreign central bank, we use volume-weighting to aggregate the holding periods across different bonds. We then take the median holding period across different foreign central banks to arrive at an estimate for the entire sector.

Chart 2 compares the estimated holding periods for foreign central banks and for other types of market participants. Foreign central banks have the longest estimated holding period, around four months, suggesting that they exhibit the strongest buy-and-hold behaviour. This could be related to central banks placing less importance on generating returns because their investment objectives differ from other types of asset managers. In turn, this could lead to less trading activity and, consequently, longer holding periods

Chart 2: Foreign central banks have longer estimated holding periods than other asset managers

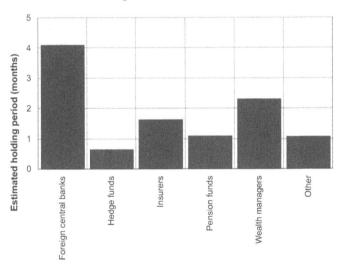

Note: *Wealth managers* includes firms that offer mutual funds, exchange-traded funds and other pooled investment products. *Other* includes non-financial corporations, credit unions and other clients of dealers.
Sources: Market Trade Reporting System and Bank of Canada calculations
Last observation: June 10, 2024

Foreign central banks lend out a small share of their holdings in the repo market

Buy-and-hold investors could offset any negative impacts their behaviour has on market liquidity if they lend their securities to other participants in securities-financing markets. To see the extent to which foreign central banks do this, we use repo transaction data from MTRS to calculate the amount of GoC bonds that foreign central banks lend out in the repo market, also known as their gross repo position.

Chart 3 shows that foreign central banks lent, on average, around $6 billion of their GoC bonds on any given day from June 2023 to June 2024. The gross repo position of foreign central banks is significantly smaller than that of pension funds and hedge funds, and slightly smaller than that of wealth managers. Insurers and other types of market participants have minimal positions. For foreign central banks, their gross repo position roughly amounts to only between 0% and 4% of their total GoC bond holdings, depending on the estimation approach used.

Chart 3: Foreign central banks' gross repo position is smaller than some other asset managers

Average daily amount from June 10, 2023–June 10, 2024

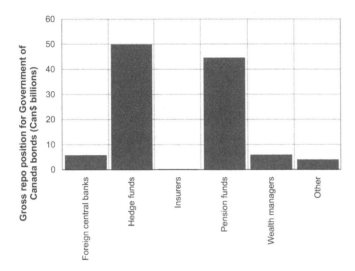

Note: *Wealth managers* includes firms that offer mutual funds, exchange-traded funds and other pooled investment products. *Other* includes non-financial corporations, credit unions and other clients of dealers.
Sources: Market Trade Reporting System and Bank of Canada calculations
Last observation: June 10, 2024

Some foreign central banks may lend their GoC bonds in the securities lending market rather than through the repo market. Foreign central banks that use the Bank of Canada as their custodian likely do not lend their securities. We are, however, unable to measure the securities lending activity of foreign central banks that use other custodians. One reason foreign central banks may have limited securities financing activity is that Canadian dollar assets represent a minimal share of their total portfolios. As a result, the incremental returns from greater securities-financing activity in Canadian markets may not be worth the operating costs for these foreign central banks relative to the returns they could earn from lending out assets denominated in other currencies. Combined with longer holding periods, their limited activity in securities-financing markets observed in our available data suggests that foreign central banks could cause liquidity to worsen in secondary markets for GoC bonds.

Bonds held by foreign central banks tend to be more illiquid

We identify cases of illiquidity in the GoC bond market from the Bank's SRO program, which aimed to support liquidity in securities-financing markets when it was active from July 2020 until October 2024. Through the SRO program, the Bank was able to lend its GoC securities to primary dealers at a slight backstop rate. Given certain terms and restrictions of the program, primary dealers would have been most incentivized to borrow bonds if they were especially illiquid in secondary markets.

Using daily bond-level data, we run a simple linear regression to assess how different factors relate to SRO volumes. We consider a short list of factors that could explain volumes in the SRO program. These factors include bond characteristics like their time to maturity or benchmark status, and program parameters like pricing and bidding limits. We also consider the GoC bond holdings of foreign central banks using custody data because the time series is more accurate than the MTRS data, where transactions are accumulated over time to estimate holdings.

Table 1 reports the coefficients and significance of each factor in the model. Our results indicate the following:

- In line with the expected relationship between the factors and liquidity, bonds with higher SRO volumes tend to:
    - have lower floats
    - be benchmark bonds
    - have longer maturities
    - have shorter tenors
- The holdings of foreign central banks have a positive and statistically significant relationship with SRO volumes. That is, an increase of Can$1 billion in foreign central banks' holdings of a given GoC bond is, on average, associated with an increase of Can$220 million in SRO volumes for that bond.

Table 1: Regression model on Securities Repo Operation volumes

Independent variable	Coefficient and significance
Foreign central bank holdings (billions)	0.22***
Float (billions)	-0.04***
Dummy for benchmark status	0.37***
Time to maturity (years)	0.01***
Tenor (years)	-0.01***
Maximum bid spread (basis points)	-0.09***
Maximum bid limit (billions)	-0.02***
Constant	1.53***
Number of observations	45,341
R-squared	0.210

Note: All regression variables are statistically significant at the 1% level (***).

While we cannot conclude whether foreign central banks are causing illiquidity or simply purchasing bonds that are already more illiquid, our results show that their holdings are related to low liquidity. If foreign central banks were to increasingly lend their GoC bonds in securities-financing markets, it may reduce the need for programs like the SRO and improve liquidity conditions independent of the Bank's programs. As an example, the Bank has a securities-lending program that makes US Treasury securities available for lending from Canada's foreign exchange reserves to enhance returns, while also supporting market liquidity.

Conclusion

We estimate that foreign central banks own a significant share of the float of GoC bonds, ranging from at least 12% to 21%. They tend to also hold their GoC bonds for longer than other market participants. Although this buy-and-hold behaviour can promote stability in periods of turmoil, it could reduce the availability of GoC bonds in secondary markets, potentially lowering liquidity. Indeed, foreign central banks lend only a small share of their bonds in the repo market—another sign of buy-and-hold behaviour.

We also find that higher holdings of GoC bonds by foreign central banks are related to illiquidity in the GoC bond market. This is because the level of these holdings has a positive and statistically significant relationship with volumes in the Bank's SRO program. Nevertheless, foreign central banks' participation in the GoC bond market brings several important benefits, such as promoting stability in periods of turmoil.

Appendix

Robustness of holding period results

To calculate holding periods, we consider only bonds that were bought and sold or had matured between August 1, 2020, and June 10, 2024. We exclude any unmatched transactions, meaning bonds that were sold but not bought or that were bought but not sold or matured. Compared with other types of market participants, foreign central banks had a significantly larger share of transactions that were unmatched and therefore excluded when calculating the holding period. Unmatched transactions indicate holding periods that may extend beyond our sample period, meaning that foreign central banks may have even longer holding periods than our calculations suggest.

Robustness of regression results

We consider two alternative methods to validate the approach we use to measure the relationship between foreign central banks' holdings of GoC bonds and liquidity. Results of these methods show that our overall conclusions hold. The two alternative methods are the following:

- We run the same regression on SRO volumes but include fixed effects for each bond and for each day. These fixed effects offer stricter ways to control for any differences between bonds and across days compared with our original model. Using this alternative regression model, we find that foreign central banks' GoC bond holdings continue to have a positive and statistically significant relationship with SRO volumes.
- We also consider a regression model where we use a different metric of illiquidity instead of SRO volumes. In this model, the dependent variable is the repo spread, which is the difference between the Canadian Overnight Repo Rate Average and the volume-weighted average repo rate for each bond on each day. Higher repo spreads indicate that a bond borrower in a repo agreement is foregoing interest income to borrow the bond, suggesting that the bond may be scarce or illiquid. Our results generally remain consistent in this alternative model.

References

Bédard-Pagé, G., D. Bolduc-Zuluaga, A. Demers, J.-P. Dion, M. Pandey, L. Berger-Soucy and Adrian Walton. 2021. "**COVID-19 crisis: Liquidity Management at Canada's Largest Public Pension Funds.**" Bank of Canada Staff Analytical Note No. 2021-11.

Feunou, B., J.-S. Fontaine, J. Kyeong and J. Sierra. 2015. "**Foreign Flows and Their Effects on Government of Canada Yields.**" Bank of Canada Staff Analytical Note No. 2015-1.

International Monetary Fund. 2024. "**Currency Composition of Official Foreign Exchange Reserves.**"

Lane, T. 2019. "**Taking Precautions: The Canadian Approach to Foreign Reserves Management.**" Speech to the Peterson Institute for International Economics, Washington, D.C., February 6.

Pomorski, L., F. Rivadeneyra and E. Wolfe. 2014. "**The Canadian Dollar as a Reserve Currency.**" *Bank of Canada Review* (Spring): 1–11.

Sandhu, J. and R. Vala. 2023. "**Do Hedge Funds Support Liquidity in the Government of Canada Bond Market?**" Bank of Canada Staff Analytical Note No. 2023-11.

Acknowledgements

We thank Cassie Davies, Jean-Philippe Dion, Jeffrey Gao, Alexandra Lai, Stéphane Lavoie, Philippe Muller, Andreas Uthemann, Adrian Walton and Jonathan Witmer for helpful comments. We are also grateful to Rishi Vala for analytical support and to Christina Harvey and Manu Pandey for data support.

Endnotes

1. For simplicity, we consider foreign central banks to be central banks or authorities other than the Bank of Canada that manage foreign exchange reserves.[←]

2. For instance, **Feunou et al. (2015)** estimate that foreign purchases of approximately Can$150 billion worth of GoC bonds lowered the 10-year yield by 100 basis points between 2009 and 2012, which reduced the cost of funding for the federal government. [←]

3. Our estimates of foreign central banks' GoC bond holdings are smaller than the total levels of foreign reserve assets held in Canadian dollars reported by the International Monetary Fund. These differences likely arise from the limitations of our data and from exposures to other Canadian assets that foreign central banks are investing in, which is outside of the scope of our analysis. For instance, foreign central banks may also hold GoC treasury bills, securities issued by Canadian provinces or other Canadian securities. [←]

Reprinted with the permission of the Bank of Canada, 2025.

Introduction

The 2025 edition of FP Bonds – Government, the tenth to be published by Grey House Publishing Canada, lists outstanding publicly and privately held debt securities, together with their features and provisions, issued by the Government of Canada, the provinces and selected federal and provincial agencies. All issues and amounts outstanding are as of Mar. 31, 2025, unless otherwise indicated. A Call Table appears at the end of each section listing the next call date and price for all callable bonds issued by the federal/provincial government or one of its agencies. An additional table lists all outstanding Eurobonds (Euro debt). Economic data on Canada and the provinces are provided as well as notes on Canadian taxation.

The formats for the three tables are as follows:

Main Body
- Cpn (%) – coupon rate (see Legend)
- Maturity date
- Frequency – frequency of interest payments (see Legend)
- Series
- CUSIP – CUSIP number
- Type – type of debt issued (see Legend)
- Year – year(s) of issue
- Amount (000) – total amount issued in original currency (see Legend)
- Outstanding Amount (000) - amount outstanding at Mar. 31, 2025, unless otherwise indicated
- Ref. Notes – numbered references which appear after the Call Table

Call Table
- Coupon Rate (%) – coupon rate (see Legend)
- Maturity date
- Next Call Date – date of next redemption
- Next Call Price – price at next redemption period
- Call Flag – flag indicating frequency of redemption
  - A (annual) – callable by the issuer on the day indicated and annually thereafter
  - C (continuous) – callable by issuer on or after Next Call Date
  - D (discrete) – callable by issuer on the day indicated
  - P (payment dates) – callable on day indicated plus subsequent interest payment dates

Eurobonds Table
- Cpn (%) – coupon rate (see Legend)
- Maturity date
- Frequency – frequency of interest payments (see Legend)
- Series
- Year – year(s) of issue
- Amount (000) – total amount issued in original currency (see Legend)
- Outstanding Amount (000) - amount outstanding at Mar. 31, 2025, unless otherwise indicated

Bond Ratings by Dominion Bond Rating Service are included on each issuer's title page.

Newly added front matter for this edition includes a look at the Bank of Canada's use of quantitative easing (QE) during the COVID-19 pandemic, a theoretical look at adopting an all-to-all market structure to improve the resilience of government bond markets during periods of turmoil, and an examination of the trading behaviour of foreign central banks and its potential impact on liquidity in the Government of Canada bond market.

Provincial Underwriters
Who takes which province to the market?

Province	Managers ■
Alberta	BMO-NB /CIBC/ /RBC-DS/S/TD (rotating lead managers)
British Columbia	BMO-NB /CIBC/ /RBC-DS/S/TD (rotating lead managers)
Manitoba	CIBC (lead manager)
	BMO-NB/RBC-DS (co-managers)
New Brunswick	BMO-NB/RBC-DS (rotating lead managers)
Newfoundland	RBC-DS/S (rotating lead managers)
	BMO-NB/CIBC/ML (co-managers)
Nova Scotia	BMO-NB/CIBC/RBC-DS/S (rotating lead managers)
Ontario	BMO-NB/CIBC/ML/ RBC-DS/S/TD (rotating lead managers)
P.E.I.	RBC-DS/S (rotating lead managers)
Québec	NBF (lead manager)
	BMO-NB/CIBC/ML/ RBC-DS/S (co-managers)
Saskatchewan	CIBC/RBC-DS (rotating lead managers)
	BMO-NB/S/TD (co-managers)

■ Managers are listed in alphabetical order; that may not be the same as participation in the account. Many of the managers are supported by other houses in underwriting the issues. The abbreviations above stand for:
BMO-NB– BMO Nesbitt Burns; CIBC – CIBC World Markets; ML – Merrill Lynch; NBF – National Bank Financial; RBC-DS – RBC Dominion Securities; S – Scotia Capital; TD – TD Securities.

British Columbia selects a lead for each deal, along with 2 co-leads, from BMO-NB, CIBC, RBC-DS, S and TD.

New Brunswick – One of CIBC, ML, NBF, S or TD is selected to join as a co-manager on each transaction.

Ontario selects a lead for each deal, along with 2 co-leads, from BMO-NB, CIBC, ML, RBC-DS, S and TD

Legend

Currency:
A$	Australian dollars	S$	Singapore dollars
Ch¥	Chinese Yuan (offshore)	SFr	Swiss francs
Cn¥	Chinese Yuan (onshore)	SKr	Swedish Krona
HK$	Hong Kong dollars	US$	United States dollars
Jp¥	Japanese yen	€	Euros
Nkr	Norwegian Krone	£	British pound
NZ$	New Zealand dollars		

Debt Type:
BD	Bonds	MB	Mortgage Bonds
DB	Debentures	MN	Medium Term Notes
DN	Deposit Notes	NT	Notes
EN	Equity-linked Notes	SB	Serial Bonds
LN	Loans	SV	Savings Bonds

Frequency:
A	Annually	S	Semiannually
M	Monthly		
Q	Quarterly		

Rate:
F.R.	Floating Rate	Z.R.	Zero Coupon Rate
V.R.	Variable Rate		
Var	Various		

Call Flag:
A	Annual	D	Discrete
C	Continuous	P	Payment Dates

Canadian Taxation

The following information, compiled from legislation, regulations, Department of Finance announcements and other published sources, is designed to give an outline of the various tax levies in Canada that, as of May 31, 2002 affect investments in debt obligations of or guaranteed by the Canadian Federal or Provincial Governments. Because the statutory provisions relating to the taxation of interest income and capital gains in Canada contain many special rules, all of which cannot be covered in this outline, the publisher and the author make no representation as to the accuracy or completeness of any of the following comments. Taxpayers are urged to consult their own tax advisors for advice relating to their own circumstances.

Government of Canada

Income Tax

(a) Residents of Canada

Under the federal Income Tax Act, in computing income for tax purposes, residents of Canada (individuals and corporations) must include all amounts received or receivable in respect of interest depending on the method regularly used by the taxpayer in calculating profit. Notwithstanding this general rule, taxpayers are required to include accrued interest annually on debt obligations to the extent not otherwise included in income.

Issuers of registered bonds or debentures are required to provide each year to the holders of their debt obligations a form (T-5 Supplementary) reporting the total payments of interest for that year or total interest accrued to the applicable anniversary date, as the case may be.

When a debt obligation is transferred, the transferor is required to include in income the interest accrued to the date of transfer and the transferee is allowed a corresponding deduction to the extent that such interest was otherwise included in the transferee's income.

One-half of capital gains from the sale of property, including securities, must be included in income of Canadian residents. One-half of realized capital losses may be deducted from the taxable portion of capital gains. There is provision for applying allowable capital losses against taxable capital gains of previous and subsequent taxation years. As a general rule, the gain realized by an investor on the maturity of a publicly traded interest bearing debt obligation purchased at a discount is a capital gain.

Investment dealers and financial institutions are required to recognize accrued gains and losses annually on their portfolio investments .

Discounts on interest bearing debt obligations issued by tax exempt entities, governments or other public bodies or non-residents not carrying on business in Canada will be income in the hands of the first Canadian resident non-exempt holder of such obligations if the effective yield exceeds the rate of interest by more than one-third in the case of obligations issued after June 18, 1971 and if the rate of interest is less than 5% in the case of obligations issued after December 20, 1960 and before June 19, 1971.

The Income Tax Regulations deem interest to accrue on non-interest bearing debt obligations (including stripped bonds) based on the yield. Those regulations also deem adjustments to the principal amount of indexed debt obligations (defined as obligations that are adjusted for changes in the purchasing power of money) to be interest.

Debt obligations that are convertible into shares or other debt obligations may qualify for rollover treatment so that no gain or loss would be realized on conversion.

There is a deemed disposition at fair market value of all capital property held by an individual on death. This may give rise to taxable capital gains and allowable capital losses. In the case of bequests to a spouse, or to a spouse trust, any such gains or losses may be postponed until the spouse disposes of the property. There is a similar deemed disposition in respect of specified capital property held by a resident of Canada upon becoming a non-resident.

Debt obligations of Canadian federal, provincial or municipal governments are eligible investments for registered retirement savings plans and other deferred income plans.

(b) Non-residents of Canada

The Income Tax Act provides for a withholding tax of 25% on interest (subject to certain exemptions) paid by a Canadian resident to any non-resident. This rate is reduced to 10% or 15% on payments to residents of most countries which have entered into tax treaties with Canada. The rate will depend upon the treaty. If the amount initially withheld and remitted on account of tax to the Receiver General at the time an interest payment is made to a non-resident exceeds the amount of tax payable (as limited by the appropriate tax treaty), the non-resident payee may apply to the Minister of National Revenue for a refund of the overpayment.

Debt obligations which are exempt from the withholding provisions on interest payments to non-residents include the following:

1. Bonds of or guaranteed by the Government of Canada issued on or before December 20, 1960.
2. Debt obligations of or guaranteed by Canadian federal, provincial and municipal governments issued after April 15, 1966.
3. Debt obligations of certain Canadian educational institutions, hospitals or government controlled corporations, commissions or associations issued after April 15, 1966.
4. Debt obligations issued before December 20, 1960, where the interest is neither payable in Canadian currency, nor by reference to Canadian currency.
5. Debt obligations issued after June 23, 1975 by corporations resident in Canada where the issue meets certain conditions respecting repayment.

Coupons on such tax exempt obligations issued after July 14, 1966 bear the designation "F". Coupons on obligations that are not exempt from withholding tax bear the designation "TX" if issued between March 29, 1961 and December 4, 1963, and the designation "AX" if issued after December 4, 1963. Anyone redeeming coupons on non-exempt obligations must withhold and remit to the Receiver General the appropriate amount on account of tax. There is also an exemption for interest paid by a prescribed financial institution that is the lender of an exempt government debt obligation under a securities lending arrangement.

The rate of withholding tax applicable to debt obligations of or guaranteed by a Province is 5% for issues on or before December 20, 1960 and for certain replacement issues subsequent to that date.

Trusts and organizations that are exempt from tax in their country of residence and that would be exempt if resident in Canada may obtain a certificate of exemption covering interest on debt obligations issued by arm's length obligors. Trusts or corporations which administer pension funds and charitable organizations may obtain such certificates of exemption even if they would not have exempt status in Canada provided they have exempt status in their country of residence.

Generally, unless debt obligations are used in the course of carrying on a business in Canada, a non-resident's capital gains from the disposition of a debt obligation will not be subject to Canadian income tax. However, if a non-resident sells a debt obligation to a Canadian resident at a premium above the issue price, the premium may be deemed to be a payment of interest and subject to withholding tax. Similarly, the sale of a debt obligation with accrued interest (whether actual or deemed) may result in a portion of the sale price being deemed to be a payment of interest to the extent of that accrued interest.

A non-resident of Canada may be able to claim the Canadian non-resident withholding tax as a credit against income taxes payable in his country of residence.

The Canada-United States Income Tax Convention contains a provision whereby the Canadian income of United States religious, scientific, literary, educational or charitable organizations is exempt from Canadian withholding tax to the extent that such income is exempt from income tax in the United States.

(c) Tax Treaties

The Government of Canada has negotiated or renegotiated tax treaties with the United States, United Kingdom, Algeria, Argentina, Australia, Austria, Bangladesh, Barbados, Belgium, Brazil, Bulgaria, Cameroon, Chile, China, Croatia, Cyprus, Czech Republic, Denmark, Dominican Republic, Egypt, Estonia, Finland, France, Germany, Guyana, Hungary, Iceland, India, Indonesia, Ireland, Israel, Italy, Ivory Coast, Jamaica, Japan, Jordan, Kazakhstan, Kenya, Kyrgyzstan, Latvia, Lebanon, Lithuania, Luxembourg, Malaysia, Malta, Mexico, Morocco, Netherlands, New Zealand, Nigeria, Norway, Pakistan, Papua New Guinea, Philippines, Poland, Portugal, Romania, Russian Federation, Singapore, Slovakia, South Africa, South Korea, Spain, Sri Lanka, Sweden, Switzerland, Tanzania, Thailand, Trinidad and Tobago, Tunisia, Ukraine, Uzbekistan, Vietnam, Zambia and Zimbabwe. In some cases, the tax treaty may not have been implemented by the enabling legislation or proclaimed in force either in Canada or the other treaty country, and consequently, specific inquiries should be made with respect to recently negotiated treaties.

Estate Tax

The estate tax imposed by the Government of Canada was repealed effective January 1, 1972, and, from that date, the only Federal tax liability arising on death pertains to the liability under the Income Tax Act arising from the deemed disposition of capital property referred to above.

Goods and Services Tax

The Federal Government enacted legislation implementing the goods and services tax effective January 1, 1991. Interest on debt obligations and proceeds from the sale of debt obligations are exempt from that tax.

Provincial Governments

Income and Corporation Taxes

All of the provinces of Canada have enacted income tax statutes. Generally, whether an individual or corporation is liable to taxation under any one or more of such statutes will depend on whether or not the individual or corporation was resident in or had a permanent establishment in a province during the year.

Capital Taxes

Canada and all the Provinces, except Alberta, Newfoundland and Prince Edward Island, impose a capital tax on corporations. Subject to meeting various term and hold conditions, investments in the debt obligations of other corporations (including Crown corporations) reduce a corporation's taxable capital. Except for Manitoba and Saskatchewan, investments in government debt obligations do not reduce taxable capital.

Succession Duties

All provinces have withdrawn from the field of succession duties.

Notes prepared by Eric G. Nazzer

Canada

Prime Minister: Mark Carney, Liberal Party of Canada
Capital City: Ottawa
Area: 9,984,670 sq. kilometres

Visit these Web sites:
   Government of Canada: www.canada.gc.ca
   Export Development Canada: www.edc.ca

DBRS Bond Rating at February 28, 2025 ... AAA

	2024	2023
GDP, by inc. & expend. (at market)	$2,282,475,000,000	$2,375,770,000,000
Employed (Dec.)	20,917,400	20,324,900
Unemployed (Dec.)	1,505,500	1,243,800
Average weekly earnings (Dec.)	$1,291.17	$1,211.79
December consumer price index (2002=100)	161.2	158.3
Building permits	$143,796,370,000	$132,200,383,000
Merchandise exports	$779,014,300,000	$768,272,100,000
Merchandise imports	$786,164,000,000	$770,401,700,000
Retail sales	$803,366,671,000	$794,404,142,000
Farm cash receipts	$97,309,923	$98,576,880
Population (est. July 1)	41,288,599	40,097,761
Index of gross domestic product at market prices (2017=100)	126.7	122.9
Raw materials price index (excl. crude energy products) (annual avg., 2020=100)	140.1	135.8
Crude energy products price index (annual avg., 2020=100)	140.2	145.8
Industrial product price index, manufacturing (annual avg., 2020=100)	126.7	125.7

DIRECT DEBT
March 31, 2025

Cpn %	Maturity	Freq	Series	CUSIP	Type	Year	Issued Amount (000)	Outstanding Amount (000)	Ref. Note
GOVERNMENT OF CANADA									
1.500	2025.04.01	S		135087N34	BD	2022	$12,000,000	$11,875,000	
2.875	2025.04.28	S		135087N75	BD	2022	US$3,500,000	US$3,500,000	
3.750	2025.05.01	S		135087Q31	BD	2023	$15,250,000	$15,250,000	
9.000	2025.06.01	S	A76	135087VH4	BD	'94-'96	$8,900,000	$2,133,858	
2.250	2025.06.01	S	D507	135087D50	BD	'14-'15	$13,100,000	$12,900,000	
3.500	2025.08.01	S		135087Q64	BD	2023	$19,000,000	$11,597,000	
0.500	2025.09.01	S	K940	135087K94	BD	2020	$47,500,000	$47,422,000	
3.000	2025.10.01	S		135087P24	BD	2022	$10,000,000	$10,000,000	
4.500	2025.11.01	S		135087Q80	BD	2023	$19,750,000	$19,175,000	
4.500	2026.02.01	S		135087R22	BD	'23-'24	$23,000,000	$22,250,000	
0.250	2026.03.01	S	L518	135087L51	BD	'20-'21	$34,000,000	$33,800,000	
3.000	2026.04.01	S		135087P81	BD	2023	$10,000,000	$10,000,000	
4.000	2026.05.01	S		135087R55	BD	2024	$26,000,000	$25,200,000	
0.750	2026.05.19	S		427028AB1	BD	2021	US$3,500,000	US$3,500,000	
1.500	2026.06.01	S	E679	135087E67	BD	'15-'16	$13,500,000	$13,472,000	
4.000	2026.08.01	S		135087R97	BD	2024	$22,000,000	$21,050,000	
1.000	2026.09.01	S	L930	135087L93	BD	2021	$23,000,000	$22,533,000	
3.250	2026.11.01	S		135087S39	BD	2024	$21,000,000	$21,500,000	
4.250	2026.12.01	S	VS05	135087VS0	BD	'95-'98	$5,250,000	$5,250,000	1
3.000	2027.02.01	S		135087S54	BD	'24-'25	$27,500,000	$27,500,000	
1.250	2027.03.01	S		135087M84	BD	'21-'22	$17,000,000	$17,000,000	
2.750	2027.05.01	S		135087S88	BD	2025	$16,500,000	$28,500,000	
1.000	2027.06.01	S	F825	135087F82	BD	'16-'17	$15,000,000	$14,740,000	
8.000	2027.06.01	S	VW17	135087VW1	BD	'96-'97	$9,600,000	$3,620,841	
3.245	2027.08.24	S		135087P73	BD	2022	$500,000	$500,000	2
2.750	2027.09.01	S		135087N83	BD	2022	$16,000,000	$16,000,000	
3.500	2028.03.01	S		135087P57	BD	'22-'23	$15,000,000	$15,000,000	
3.750	2028.04.26	S		135087Q56	BD	2023	US$4,000,000	US$4,000,000	
2.000	2028.06.01	S	H235	135087H23	BD	'17-'18	$13,500,000	$13,500,000	
3.250	2028.09.01	S		135087Q49	BD	2023	$20,000,000	$20,000,000	
4.000	2029.03.01	S		135087Q98	BD	'23-'24	$27,000,000	$27,000,000	
4.625	2029.04.30	S		43358BAA1	BD	2024	US$3,000,000	US$3,000,000	
2.250	2029.06.01	S	J397	135087J39	BD	'18-'19	$12,300,000	$12,300,000	
5.750	2029.06.01	S	WL43	135087WL4	BD	'98-'01	$13,900,000	$10,598,959	
3.500	2029.09.01	S		135087R89	BD	2024	$30,000,000	$30,000,000	
2.250	2029.12.01	S		135087N67	BD	2022	$5,000,000	$5,000,000	3
2.750	2030.03.01	S		135087S47	BD	'24-'25	$33,000,000	$33,000,000	
4.000	2030.03.18	S		43358BAB9	BD	2025	US$3,500,000	US$3,500,000	
1.250	2030.06.01	S	K379	135087K37	BD	'19-'20	$44,200,000	$44,200,000	
0.500	2030.12.01	S	L443	135087L44	BD	'20-'21	$40,000,000	$40,000,000	
1.500	2031.06.01	S	M276	135087M27	BD	2021	$42,000,000	$42,000,000	
1.500	2031.12.01	S		135087N26	BD	'21-'22	$32,000,000	$32,000,000	
4.000	2031.12.01	S	WV25	135087WV2	BD	'99-'03	$5,800,000	$5,800,000	1
3.000	2032.03.01	S		135087S96	BD	2025	$2,000,000	$2,000,000	3
2.000	2032.06.01	S		135087N59	BD	2022	$24,000,000	$24,000,000	
2.500	2032.12.01	S		135087P32	BD	2022	$21,000,000	$21,000,000	

FP Bonds — Government 2025

Canada

Cpn %	Maturity	Freq	Series	CUSIP	Type	Year	Issued Amount (000)	Outstanding Amount (000)	Ref. Note
2.750	2033.06.01	S		135087Q23	BD	2023	$19,000,000	$19,000,000	
5.750	2033.06.01	S	XG49	135087XG4	BD	'01-'04	$13,410,295	$11,988,905	
3.250	2033.12.01	S		135087Q72	BD	2023	$21,000,000	$21,000,000	
3.500	2034.03.01	S		135087R71	BD	2024	$6,000,000	$6,000,000	3
3.000	2034.06.01	S		135087R48	BD	'23-'24	$34,000,000	$34,000,000	
3.250	2034.12.01	S		135087S21	BD	2024	$30,000,000	$30,000,000	
3.250	2035.06.01	S		135087S62	BD	2025	$18,000,000	$28,500,000	
3.000	2036.12.01	S	XQ21	135087XQ2	BD	'03-'07	$5,850,000	$5,850,000	1
5.000	2037.06.01	S	XW98	135087XW9	BD	'04-'09	$13,999,089	$11,730,774	
4.000	2041.06.01	S	YQ12	135087YQ1	BD	'08-'11	$15,800,000	$13,838,441	
2.000	2041.12.01	S	YK42	13522ZYK4	BD	'07-'10	$6,550,000	$6,550,000	1
1.500	2044.12.01	S	ZH04	135087ZH0	BD	'10-'13	$7,700,000	$7,700,000	1
3.500	2045.12.01	S	ZS68	135087ZS6	BD	'11-'14	$16,400,000	$16,300,000	
1.250	2047.12.01	S	B949	135087B94	BD	'13-'17	$7,700,000	$7,700,000	1
2.750	2048.12.01	S	D358	135087D35	BD	'14-'17	$14,900,000	$14,900,000	
0.500	2050.12.01	S	G997	135087G99	BD	'17-'21	$7,600,000	$7,600,000	1
2.000	2051.12.01	S	H722	135087H72	BD	'17-'21	$49,700,000	$51,816,529	
1.750	2053.12.01	S		135087M68	BD	'21-'22	$32,000,000	$32,000,000	
0.250	2054.12.01	S		135087M43	BD	'21-'22	$2,100,000	$2,100,000	
2.750	2055.12.01	S		135087P99	BD	'23-'24	$28,750,000	$28,750,000	
3.500	2057.12.01	S		135087S70	BD	2025	$5,000,000	$8,000,000	
2.750	2064.12.01	S	C939	135087C93	BD	'14-'22	$8,750,000	$8,750,000	

GUARANTEED DEBT
March 31, 2025

Cpn %	Maturity	Freq	Series	CUSIP	Type	Year	Issued Amount (000)	Outstanding Amount (000)	Ref. Note
CPPIB CAPITAL INC.									
F.R.	2025.04.04	Q	47	22411WAU0	NT	2022	US$1,500,000	US$1,500,000	
6.000	2025.06.07	A	58		NT	2023	£1,000,000	£1,000,000	
0.375	2025.07.29	S	26	22411VAP3	NT	2020	US$1,000,000	US$1,000,000	
3.950	2025.09.08	S	53	C28009AF2	NT	2022	$500,000	$500,000	
4.400	2026.01.16	S			NT	'23-'24	A$1,500,000	A$1,500,000	
4.375	2026.03.02	A	56		SN	2023	£750,000	£750,000	
F.R.	2026.03.11	Q	40	12593CAQ4	SN	2021	US$750,000	US$750,000	
F.R.	2026.06.15	Q	37		NT	2021	£750,000	£750,000	
F.R.	2026.07.27	Q	66	22411VBB3	NT	2024	US$500,000	US$500,000	
4.100	2026.09.01	S	4		MN	2023	A$500,000	A$500,000	
0.875	2026.09.09	S	42	22411VAU2	MN	2021	US$2,500,000	US$2,500,000	
4.375	2027.01.31	S	62	22411VBA5	NT	2024	US$1,250,000	US$1,250,000	
0.250	2027.04.06	A	19		MN	2020	€1,000,000	€1,000,000	
F.R.	2027.04.27	Q	49		SN	2022	£300,000	£300,000	
2.850	2027.06.01	S	48	12593CAT8	NT	2022	$1,500,000	$1,500,000	
3.250	2027.06.15	S	51	22411WAW6	NT	2022	US$1,500,000	US$1,500,000	
4.700	2027.07.19	S			NT	2024	A$1,000,000	A$1,000,000	
4.500	2027.07.22	A	63		NT	2024	£600,000	£600,000	
4.450	2027.09.01	S			NT	'22-'23	A$1,350,000	A$1,350,000	
3.750	2027.10.08	S	67	22411VBC1	NT	2024	US$1,750,000	US$1,750,000	

Cpn %	Maturity	Freq	Series	CUSIP	Type	Year	Issued Amount (000)	Outstanding Amount (000)	Ref. Note
2.750	2027.11.02	S	4	22411VAD0	NT	2017	US$1,000,000	US$1,000,000	
1.250	2027.12.07	A	44		MN	2022	£600,000	£600,000	
3.250	2028.03.08	S	57	12593CAV3	NT	2023	$3,000,000	$3,000,000	
4.200	2028.05.02	S			NT	2023	A$1,600,000	A$1,600,000	
3.000	2028.06.15	S	8	12593CAF8	NT	'18-'22	$2,500,000	$2,500,000	
1.500	2028.06.23	S	38		NT	2021	A$750,000	A$750,000	
4.250	2028.07.20	S	59	22411VAZ1	NT	2023	US$1,500,000	US$1,500,000	
4.400	2029.01.15	S			NT	2024	A$1,500,000	A$1,500,000	
0.875	2029.02.06	A	12		NT	2019	€1,000,000	€1,000,000	
3.600	2029.06.02	S	61	12593CAX9	NT	2024	$3,000,000	$3,000,000	
3.125	2029.06.11	A	65		NT	2024	€1,000,000	€1,000,000	
1.950	2029.09.30	S	14	12593CAJ0	BD	2019	$1,000,000	$1,000,000	
2.000	2029.11.01	S	15	22411WAK2	NT	2019	US$1,000,000	US$1,000,000	
1.125	2029.12.14	A	23		SN	2020	£750,000	£750,000	
4.600	2030.01.16	S			NT	2025	A$2,500,000	A$2,500,000	
3.350	2030.12.02	S	68	12593CBA8	NT	2025	$2,250,000	$2,250,000	
1.250	2031.01.28	S	29	22411WAQ9	NT	2021	US$1,000,000	US$1,000,000	
0.050	2031.02.24	A	31		MN	2021	€1,000,000	€1,000,000	
2.250	2031.12.01	S	45	12593CAR2	NT	2022	$1,400,000	$1,400,000	
2.875	2032.01.30	A	69		NT	2025	€1,250,000	€1,250,000	
3.950	2032.06.02	S	55	12593ZAA8	NT	2023	$3,700,000	$3,700,000	
1.500	2033.03.04	A	6		NT	2018	€1,000,000	€1,000,000	
4.750	2033.06.02	S	60	12593CAW1	NT	'23-'24	$3,000,000	$3,000,000	
5.200	2034.03.04	S			NT	2024	A$1,500,000	A$1,500,000	
4.300	2034.06.02	S	64	12593CAY7	NT	'24-'25	$3,000,000	$3,500,000	
0.750	2037.02.02	A	46		MN	2022	€1,000,000	€1,000,000	
0.250	2041.01.18	A	28		NT	2021	€1,000,000	€1,000,000	
2.414	2041.02.25	S			MN	2021	A$150,000	A$150,000	
2.790	2041.03.12	S	33		MN	2021	A$120,000	A$120,000	
2.565	2041.04.23	A			MN	2021	A$110,000	A$110,000	
0.750	2049.07.15	A	13		NT	2019	€1,000,000	€1,000,000	
2.580	2051.02.23	S	30		MN	2021	A$160,000	A$160,000	
1.625	2071.10.22	A	43		NT	2021	£900,000	£900,000	

CPPIB REAL ESTATE HOLDINGS INC.

Cpn %	Maturity	Freq	Series	CUSIP	Type	Year	Issued Amount (000)	Outstanding Amount (000)	Ref. Note
3.752	2025.06.10	M	A	12593EAA5	MB	2015	$175,000	$131,225	

CANADA HOUSING TRUST

Cpn %	Maturity	Freq	Series	CUSIP	Type	Year	Issued Amount (000)	Outstanding Amount (000)	Ref. Note
0.950	2025.06.15	S	93	13509PHN6	MB	2020	$12,000,000	$12,000,000	
F.R.	2025.09.15	Q	94	13509PHP1	MB	2020	$2,000,000	$2,000,000	
1.950	2025.12.15	S	67	13509PFA6	MB	'15-'20	$13,000,000	$13,000,000	
2.250	2025.12.15	S	70	13509PFD0	MB	'15-'16	$4,000,000	$4,000,000	
F.R.	2026.03.15	Q	96	13509PHR7	MB	'20-'21	$3,000,000	$3,000,000	
1.250	2026.06.15	S	98	13509PHT3	MB	2021	$10,000,000	$10,000,000	
1.900	2026.09.15	S	73	13509PFL2	MB	2016	$7,000,000	$7,000,000	
F.R.	2026.09.15	Q	99	13509PHV8	MB	2021	$2,250,000	$2,250,000	
1.100	2026.12.15	S	102	13509PHX4	MB	2021	$5,250,000	$5,250,000	
1.550	2026.12.15	S	105	13509PJA2	MB	2021	$5,000,000	$5,000,000	
F.R.	2027.03.15	Q	103	13509PHY2	MB	'21-'22	$2,000,000	$2,000,000	
3.800	2027.06.15	S	109	13509PJE4	MB	2022	$5,000,000	$5,000,000	
2.350	2027.06.15	S	77	13509PFX6	MB	'17-'22	$12,250,000	$12,250,000	
F.R.	2027.09.15	Q	108	13509PJD6	MB	2022	$2,500,000	$2,500,000	

FP Bonds — Government 2025

Canada

Cpn %	Maturity	Freq	Series	CUSIP	Type	Year	Issued Amount (000)	Outstanding Amount (000)	Ref. Note
3.600	2027.12.15	S	110	13509PJF1	MB	2022	$10,000,000	$10,000,000	
F.R.	2028.03.15	Q	111	13509PJG9	MB	'22-'23	$2,500,000	$2,500,000	
2.350	2028.03.15	S	80	13509PGF4	MB	2017	$2,500,000	$2,500,000	
2.650	2028.03.15	S	82	13509PGL1	MB	2018	$4,250,000	$4,250,000	
3.100	2028.06.15	S	113	13509PJL8	MB	2023	$5,000,000	$5,000,000	
3.950	2028.06.15	S	115	13509PJN4	MB	2023	$5,000,000	$5,000,000	
F.R.	2028.09.15	Q	114	13509PJM6	MB	2023	$2,250,000	$2,250,000	
4.250	2028.12.15	S	117	13509PJQ7	MB	2023	$11,000,000	$11,000,000	
2.650	2028.12.15	S	85	13509PGS6	MB	'18-'19	$6,500,000	$6,500,000	
F.R.	2029.03.15	Q	119	13509PJR5	MB	'23-'24	$1,000,000	$1,000,000	
3.700	2029.06.15	S	120	13509PJT1	MB	2024	$16,000,000	$16,000,000	
F.R.	2029.09.15	Q	121	13509PJU8	MB	2024	$1,000,000	$1,000,000	
2.100	2029.09.15	S	88	13509PHD8	MB	2019	$6,750,000	$6,750,000	
2.900	2029.12.15	S	123	13509PJX2	MB	2024	$15,000,000	$15,000,000	
F.R.	2030.03.15	Q	124	13509PJZ7	MB	'24-'25	$1,500,000	$1,500,000	
2.850	2030.06.15	S	126	13509PKC6	MB	2025	$8,500,000	$8,500,000	
1.750	2030.06.15	S	92	13509PHM8	MB	2020	$10,750,000	$10,750,000	
1.900	2031.03.15	S	100	13509PHU0	MB	2021	$3,500,000	$3,500,000	
1.100	2031.03.15	S	95	13509PHQ9	MB	2020	$4,250,000	$4,250,000	
1.400	2031.03.15	S	97	13509PHS5	MB	2021	$4,000,000	$4,000,000	
1.600	2031.12.15	S	101	13509PHW6	MB	2021	$4,000,000	$4,000,000	
2.150	2031.12.15	S	104	13509PHZ9	MB	2021	$4,000,000	$4,000,000	
2.450	2031.12.15	S	106	13509PJB0	MB	2022	$3,750,000	$3,750,000	
3.550	2032.09.15	S	107	13509PJC8	MB	2022	$11,000,000	$11,000,000	
3.650	2033.06.15	S	112	13509PJK0	MB	2023	$8,000,000	$8,000,000	
4.150	2033.06.15	S	116	13509PJP9	MB	2023	$4,000,000	$4,000,000	
4.250	2034.03.15	S	118	13509PJS3	MB	'23-'24	$22,000,000	$22,000,000	
3.500	2034.12.15	S	122	13509PJW4	MB	2024	$13,000,000	$13,000,000	
3.450	2035.03.15	S	125	13509PKB8	MB	2025	$6,000,000	$6,000,000	

EXPORT DEVELOPMENT CANADA

Cpn %	Maturity	Freq	Series	CUSIP	Type	Year	Issued Amount (000)	Outstanding Amount (000)	Ref. Note
3.375	2025.08.26	S		30216BJU7	BD	2022	US$3,250,000	US$3,250,000	
2.720	2025.09.13	A			MN	2022	Ch¥1,000,000	Ch¥1,000,000	
2.600	2026.01.17	A			MN	2023	Ch¥1,000,000	Ch¥1,000,000	
1.050	2026.05.26	S		30216BJP8	NT	2021	US$200,000	US$200,000	
4.375	2026.06.29	S		30216BKB7	BD	2023	US$2,000,000	US$2,000,000	
4.400	2027.01.22	S			NT	2023	A$1,000,000	A$1,000,000	
3.000	2027.05.25	S		30216BJR4	BD	2022	US$2,750,000	US$2,750,000	
3.750	2027.09.07	S		30216BKH4	BD	2024	US$1,750,000	US$1,750,000	
3.875	2028.02.14	S		30216BJW3	BD	2023	US$3,500,000	US$3,500,000	
F.R.	2028.08.01	Q		C36025AK7	BD	2024	US$1,000,000	US$1,000,000	
4.500	2028.09.06	S			BD	2023	A$1,000,000	A$1,000,000	
4.125	2029.02.13	S		30216BKC5	NT	2024	US$3,500,000	US$3,500,000	
4.500	2029.08.08	S			NT	2024	A$1,000,000	A$1,000,000	
4.750	2034.06.05	S		30216BKF8	NT	2024	US$1,000,000	US$1,000,000	

PSP CAPITAL INC.

Cpn %	Maturity	Freq	Series	CUSIP	Type	Year	Issued Amount (000)	Outstanding Amount (000)	Ref. Note
5.250	2035.02.27	S			NT	2025	A$1,250,000	A$1,250,000	

CALLABLE BONDS

March 31, 2025

Coupon Rate %	Maturity Date	Next Call Date	Next Call Price	Call Flag
CPPIB REAL ESTATE HOLDINGS INC.				
3.752	2025.06.10	anytime	$100.00	C

REFERENCES
1. Real return bonds. The bonds bear interest adjusted in relation to the Consumer Price Index for Canada. Interest consists of both an inflation compensation component calculated based on principal and payable at maturity and a cash entitlement calculated based on principal and accrued inflation compensation. Coupon interest is payable semiannually. At maturity, in addition to coupon interest payable on such date, a final payment equal to the sum of principal plus inflation compensation accrued from the original issue date to maturity will be made.
2. Ukraine Sovereignty Bonds.
3. Green bonds.

Treasury Bills

Maturity Date 2025	Issue Date 2024	Average Price	Average Yield	Outstanding $000,000
Jan. 3	Jan. 4	95.529	4.680	4,200
Jan. 3	Jan. 18	95.698	4.675	4,400
Jan. 3	Sept. 25	98.922	3.979	12,200
Jan. 3	Dec. 4	99.712	3.509	2,500
Jan. 15	July 17	97.829	4.450	4,200
Jan. 15	July 31	98.045	4.332	4,800
Jan. 15	Oct. 9	98.958	3.920	12,800
Jan. 15	Dec. 18	99.754	3.220	2,500
Jan. 30	Feb. 1	95.456	4.773	4,400
Jan. 30	Feb. 15	95.482	4.935	5,000
Jan. 30	Oct. 23	99.022	3.643	12,800
Feb. 12	Aug. 14	97.984	4.126	5,400
Feb. 12	Aug. 28	98.157	4.080	5,200
Feb. 12	Nov. 6	99.066	3.511	13,400
Feb. 27	Feb. 29	95.422	4.811	5,000
Feb. 27	Mar. 14	95.648	4.745	5,000
Feb. 27	Nov. 20	99.065	3.481	13,100
Mar. 12	Sept. 11	98.098	3.889	5,000
Mar. 12	Sept. 25	98.296	3.766	4,400
Mar. 12	Dec. 4	99.105	3.362	12,200
Mar. 27	Mar. 28	95.486	4.740	5,600
Mar. 27	Apr. 11	95.688	4.699	5,000
Mar. 27	Dec. 18	99.154	3.147	12,800
Apr. 9	Oct. 9	98.147	3.786	4,600
Apr. 9	Oct. 23	98.392	3.550	4,600
Apr. 24	Apr. 25	95.463	4.766	4,600
Apr. 24	May 9	95.697	4.689	4,600
May 7	Nov. 6	98.327	3.412	4,800
May 7	Nov. 20	98.455	3.410	4,700
May 22	May 23	95.566	4.653	4,400
May 22	June 5	95.761	4.603	4,600
June 4	Dec. 4	98.383	3.296	4,400
June 4	Dec. 18	98.574	3.143	4,600
June 18	June 19	95.826	4.368	4,400
June 18	July 3	95.881	4.480	4,200
July 16	July 17	95.933	4.251	4,200
July 16	July 31	96.211	4.107	4,800
Aug. 13	Aug. 14	96.338	3.812	5,400
Aug. 13	Aug. 28	96.502	3.780	5,200
Sept. 10	Sept. 11	96.593	3.537	5,000
Sept. 10	Sept. 25	96.880	3.358	4,400
Oct. 8	Oct. 9	96.587	3.543	4,600
Oct. 8	Oct. 23	96.912	3.323	4,600
Nov. 5	Nov. 6	96.808	3.306	4,800
Nov. 5	Nov. 20	96.909	3.326	4,700
Dec. 3	Dec. 4	96.887	3.222	4,400
Dec. 3	Dec. 18	97.094	3.121	4,600
Total				**273,100**

Alberta

Premier: Danielle Smith (United Conservative Party)
Capital City: Edmonton
Area: 661,848 sq. kilometres

Visit these Web sites:
   Province of Alberta: www.alberta.ca
   Alberta Capital Finance Authority: www.acfa.gov.ab.ca

DBRS Bond Rating at September 13, 2024 ... AA

	2024	2023
Employed	2,572,700	2,502,600
Unemployment rate (%)	6.7	6.3
Average weekly earnings (Dec.)	$1,340.03	$1,291.41
Building permits	$18,844,906,000	$15,772,620,000
Retail sales	$103,824,845,000	$102,122,841,000
Population (est. July 1)	4,888,723	4,695,290
December consumer price index (2002=100)	169.7	165.6
Sales tax (GST)	5%	5%

FP Bonds — Government 2025

DIRECT DEBT

March 31, 2025

Cpn %	Maturity	Freq	Series	CUSIP	Type	Year	Issued Amount (000)	Outstanding Amount (000)	Ref. Note
PROVINCE OF ALBERTA									
0.500	2025.04.16	A			NT	2020	€1,100,000	€1,100,000	
0.625	2025.04.18	A			NT	2018	€1,500,000	€1,500,000	
1.000	2025.05.20	S		013051EK9	BD	2020	US$2,250,000	US$2,250,000	
2.350	2025.06.01	S	DJ	013051DQ7	DB	'15-'20	$3,700,000	$3,700,000	
0.625	2026.01.16	A			NT	2019	€1,250,000	€1,250,000	
4.300	2026.06.01	S		01306ZCP4	NT	2011	$30,000	$30,000	
2.200	2026.06.01	S		013051DT1	NT	'16-'20	$3,700,000	$3,700,000	
2.050	2026.08.17	S	PAGM06	01306GAC7	NT	2016	US$1,000,000	US$1,000,000	
3.100	2026.12.14	S			NT	'16-'18	A$505,000	A$505,000	
2.550	2027.06.01	S		013051DW4	NT	'17-'20	$5,700,000	$5,700,000	
3.300	2028.03.15	S		013051EA1	BD	2018	US$1,250,000	US$1,250,000	
3.600	2028.04.11	S			NT	'17-'19	A$460,000	A$460,000	
0.250	2028.04.20	A			NT	2020	SFr260,000	SFr260,000	
2.900	2028.12.01	S		013051EB9	DB	'18-'19	$3,300,000	$3,300,000	
0.375	2029.02.07	A			MN	2019	SFr325,000	SFr325,000	
1.403	2029.02.20	A			NT	2019	SKr2,500,000	SKr2,500,000	
4.100	2029.06.01	S		013051EU7	NT	2024	$1,000,000	$1,000,000	
4.500	2029.06.26	S		013051EV5	BD	2024	US$1,500,000	US$1,500,000	
2.900	2029.09.20	S		01306ZCV1	NT	'12-'20	$2,062,700	$2,062,700	
2.050	2030.06.01	S		013051EG8	DB	'19-'20	$8,100,000	$8,100,000	
1.300	2030.07.22	S		013051EM5	DB	2020	US$2,000,000	US$2,000,000	
2.400	2030.10.02	S			MN	2020	A$170,000	A$170,000	
3.500	2031.06.01	S		01306ZDF5	NT	2014	$1,230,000	$1,230,000	
1.650	2031.06.01	S		013051EP8	BD	2021	$3,500,000	$3,500,000	
4.150	2033.06.01	S		013051ER4	BD	'22-'24	$2,750,000	$2,750,000	
3.900	2033.12.01	S		01306ZDC2	NT	'13-'21	$1,815,000	$1,815,000	
4.500	2034.01.24	S		013051ET0	BD	2024	US$1,250,000	US$1,250,000	
5.200	2034.05.15	S			NT	2024	A$1,100,000	A$1,100,000	
3.125	2034.10.16	A			NT	2024	€1,500,000	€1,500,000	
3.950	2035.06.01	S		013051EW3	NT	'24-'25	$1,400,000	$1,400,000	
2.010	2036.02.19	S			MN	2021	A$200,000	A$200,000	
4.500	2040.12.01	S		013051DB0	BD	2010	$600,000	$600,000	
1.782	2040.12.03	A			NT	'15-'16	€202,000	€202,000	
3.225	2041.09.16	S			NT	2021	NZ$128,000	NZ$128,000	
3.450	2043.12.01	S		013051DK0	NT	'13-'15	$2,500,000	$2,500,000	
1.150	2043.12.01	A			NT	'16-'17	€435,000	€435,000	
0.925	2045.05.08	A			NT	2020	€70,000	€70,000	
2.473	2046.02.16	S			MN	2021	A$100,000	A$100,000	
3.300	2046.12.01	S		013051DS3	BD	'15-'17	$5,200,000	$5,200,000	
3.050	2048.12.01	S		013051DY0	NT	'17-'18	$6,900,000	$6,900,000	
1.413	2050.03.31	A			MN	2020	€30,000	€30,000	
1.500	2050.04.07	A			MN	2020	€90,000	€90,000	
3.100	2050.06.01	S		013051ED5	NT	'18-'21	$8,920,000	$8,920,000	
2.070	2050.12.09	S		013051EN3	NT	2020	US$39,650	US$39,650	
2.950	2052.06.01	S		013051EQ6	BD	'21-'22	$3,500,000	$3,500,000	

Cpn %	Maturity	Freq	Series	CUSIP	Type	Year	Issued Amount (000)	Outstanding Amount (000)	Ref. Note
4.450	2054.12.01	S		013051ES2	DB	'23-'25	$2,000,000	$2,000,000	
2.400	2060.06.01	S		01306ZDJ7	MN	2020	$200,000	$200,000	
2.850	2071.06.01	S		01306ZDK4	MN	2021	$125,000	$125,000	
3.060	2120.06.01	S		013051EJ2	MN	2020	$700,000	$700,000	

GUARANTEED DEBT
March 31, 2025

Cpn %	Maturity	Freq	Series	CUSIP	Type	Year	Issued Amount (000)	Outstanding Amount (000)	Ref. Note
ALBERTA CAPITAL FINANCE AUTHORITY									
4.450	2025.12.15	S	DX	01285PBU1	NT	2005	$300,000	$300,000	

British Columbia

Premier: David Eby (New Democratic Party)
Capital City: Victoria
Area: 994,735 sq. kilometres

Visit these Web sites:
    Province of British Columbia: www.gov.bc.ca
    British Columbia Investment Management Corporation: www.bci.ca

DBRS Bond Rating at April 30, 2025 ... AA high

	2024	2023
Employed	2,920,600	2,837,900
Unemployment rate (%)	5.9	5.5
Average weekly earnings (Dec.)	$1,290.29	$1,230.39
Building permits	$22,990,179,000	$22,798,443,000
Retail sales	$108,081,642,000	$108,967,837,000
Population (est. July 1)	5,698,430	5,519,013
December consumer price index (2002=100)	156.1	152.1
Sales tax (GST)	5%	5%
(PST)	7%	7%

DIRECT DEBT
March 31, 2025

Cpn %	Maturity	Freq	Series	CUSIP	Type	Issued Year	Issued Amount (000)	Outstanding Amount (000)	Ref. Note
PROVINCE OF BRITISH COLUMBIA									
2.850	2025.06.18	S	BCCD-34	11070TAF5	BD	'14-'20	$4,050,000	$4,050,000	
0.875	2025.10.08	A	BCEURO-2		BD	2015	€500,000	€500,000	
6.500	2026.01.15	S	BCUSD-2	110709DL3	BD	1996	US$500,000	US$500,000	1
2.250	2026.06.02	S	BCUSG-9	11070TAK4	BD	2016	US$750,000	US$750,000	
2.300	2026.06.18	S	BCCD-36	11070TAJ7	BD	'16-'17	$1,500,000	$1,500,000	
0.900	2026.07.20	S	BCUSG-12	110709AH5	BD	2021	US$2,500,000	US$2,500,000	
8.000	2026.09.09	S	BCMTN-63	11070ZBV5	MN	1996	$110,000	$110,000	
7.000	2026.12.04	S	BCMTN-64	11070ZBW3	MN	1996	$40,000	$40,000	
7.000	2026.12.04	S	BCMTN-74	11070ZCH5	MN	1999	$60,000	$60,000	
2.500	2027.02.26	S	BCAUD-2		NT	'16-'17	A$170,000	A$170,000	
7.500	2027.06.09	S	BCMTN-65	11070ZBX1	MN	1997	$50,000	$50,000	
2.550	2027.06.18	S	BCCD-37	11070TAL2	NT	'17-'20	$2,300,000	$2,300,000	
6.150	2027.11.19	S	BCCD-W	110709EJ7	BD	'97-'99	$500,000	$500,000	
4.700	2028.01.24	S	BCUSG-17	11070TAN8	BD	2025	US$3,500,000	US$3,500,000	
5.620	2028.08.17	S	BCMTN-70	11070ZCC6	MN	1998	$200,000	$200,000	
4.800	2028.11.15	S	BCUSG-14	110709AJ1	BD	2023	US$2,000,000	US$2,000,000	
2.950	2028.12.18	S	BCCD-38	110709GH9	BD	'18-'19	$2,000,000	$2,000,000	
4.900	2029.04.24	S	BCUSG-15	110709AL6	BD	2024	US$2,500,000	US$2,500,000	
5.150	2029.06.18	S	BCCD-14	110709FP2	BD	'07-'13	$495,000	$495,000	
5.700	2029.06.18	S	BCCD-X	110709EK4	BD	'98-'99	$2,285,000	$2,285,000	
4.500	2029.06.18	A	BCGBP-02		NT	2024	£500,000	£500,000	
5.861	2029.06.18	S	BCMTN-83	11070ZCS1	MN	1999	$250,000	$250,000	
2.500	2030.04.18	A	BCSFR-7		MN	2010	SFr100,000	SFr100,000	
2.200	2030.06.18	S	BCCD-40	110709GK2	BD	'19-'21	$4,210,000	$4,210,000	
1.300	2031.01.29	S	BCUSG-11	110709AE2	BD	2021	US$1,750,000	US$1,750,000	
5.000	2031.06.18	S	BCCD-19	110709FV9	MN	'08-'13	$1,035,000	$1,035,000	
1.550	2031.06.18	S	BCCD-41	110709AF9	BD	'21-'22	$3,800,000	$3,800,000	
6.350	2031.06.18	S	BCCD-Z	110709EX6	BD	'00-'01	$1,400,000	$1,400,000	
2.500	2032.05.16	S	BCAUD-3		MN	2021	A$70,000	A$70,000	
3.200	2032.06.18	S	BCCD-43	110709GL0	NT	'22-'23	$2,500,000	$2,500,000	
4.950	2032.07.16	S	BCAUD-6		NT	2025	A$1,000,000	A$1,000,000	
0.700	2032.07.20	A	BCEURO-5		MN	2016	€250,000	€250,000	
2.600	2032.12.14	S	BCAUD-4		MN	2021	A$78,000	A$78,000	
3.550	2033.06.18	S	BCCD-45	110709GN6	DB	'23-'24	$3,000,000	$3,000,000	
4.200	2033.07.06	S	BCUSG-13	11070TAM0	BD	2023	US$2,250,000	US$2,250,000	
5.250	2034.05.23	S	BCAUD-5		NT	2024	A$1,000,000	A$1,000,000	
4.750	2034.06.12	S	BCUSG-16	110709AN2	NT	2024	US$2,000,000	US$2,000,000	
4.150	2034.06.18	S	BCCD-46	110709AK8	BD	2024	$5,000,000	$5,000,000	
3.000	2034.07.24	A	BCEURO-17		BD	2024	€1,850,000	€1,850,000	
4.000	2035.06.18	S	BCCD-48	110709AP7	BD	2025	$2,250,000	$3,000,000	
5.400	2035.06.18	S	BCCD-7	110709FJ6	BD	2004	$500,000	$500,000	
7.250	2036.09.01	S	BCUSD-3	110709EC2	BD	1996	US$300,000	US$300,000	1
1.337	2037.01.27	A	BCEURO-6		MN	2017	€150,000	€150,000	
4.700	2037.06.18	S	BCCD-11	110709FL1	BD	'06-'08	$1,500,000	$1,500,000	
3.210	2038.11.08	A	BCEURO-1		MN	2011	€40,000	€40,000	
5.750	2039.01.09	S	BCMTN-69	11070ZCB8	MN	1998	$150,000	$150,000	

							Issued	Outstanding	Ref.
Cpn %	Maturity	Freq	Series	CUSIP	Type	Year	Amount (000)	Amount (000)	Note
6.000	2039.01.09	S	BCMTN-73	11070ZCF9	MN	1998	$65,000	$65,000	
3.741	2039.04.01	A	BCEURO-16		NT	2023	€100,000	€100,000	
3.400	2039.05.24	A	BCEURO-18		NT	2024	€1,500,000	€1,500,000	
3.508	2039.06.07	A	BCEURO-14		NT	2023	€86,000	€86,000	
2.060	2039.06.09	A	BCEURO-13		MN	2022	€100,000	€100,000	
6.300	2039.08.23	S	BCMTN-84	11070ZCT9	MN	1999	$200,000	$200,000	
4.950	2040.06.18	S	BCCD-22	110709FY3	BD	'08-'10	$2,300,000	$2,300,000	
1.678	2040.12.18	A	BCEURO-3		NT	2015	€75,000	€75,000	
4.300	2042.06.18	S	BCCD-25	1107098Y1	BD	'10-'12	$3,850,000	$3,850,000	
0.590	2042.12.22	A	BCEURO-12		MN	2021	€135,000	€135,000	
1.250	2043.06.17	A	BCEURO-4		MN	2016	€100,000	€100,000	
5.250	2043.06.18	S	BCCD-1	11070ZDD3	MN	2003	$150,000	$150,000	
1.227	2044.04.25	A	BCEURO-7		MN	2019	€130,000	€130,000	
3.200	2044.06.18	S	BCCD-29	110709GC0	DB	'12-'14	$4,100,000	$4,100,000	
5.750	2044.08.23	S	BCCD-10	11070ZDL5	MN	'04-'08	$136,000	$136,000	
4.600	2045.06.18	S	BCCD-18	110709FU1	MN	2008	$50,000	$50,000	
3.300	2046.06.28	A	BCEURO-19		NT	2024	€50,000	€50,000	
1.000	2048.04.09	A	BCEURO-11		BD	2020	€170,000	€170,000	
4.900	2048.06.18	S	BCCD-15	110709FQ0	BD	'07-'11	$555,000	$555,000	
2.800	2048.06.18	S	BCCD-35	11070TAG3	BD	'15-'18	$5,000,000	$5,000,000	
0.478	2049.10.18	A	BCEURO-9		NT	'19-'23	€709,000	€709,000	
0.270	2050.03.30	A	BCEURO-10		NT	2020	€150,000	€150,000	
2.950	2050.06.18	S	BCCD-39	110709GJ5	NT	'18-'21	$6,400,000	$6,400,000	
2.750	2052.06.18	S	BCCD-42	110709AG7	BD	'21-'22	$4,300,000	$4,300,000	
3.402	2053.06.05	A	BCEURO-15		NT	2023	€80,000	€80,000	
4.250	2053.12.18	S	BCCD-44	110709GM8	BD	'22-'24	$4,800,000	$4,800,000	
3.500	2055.06.18	S	BCCD-27	110709GA4	MN	'12-'13	$190,000	$190,000	
4.450	2055.12.18	S	BCCD-47	110709GP1	NT	'24-'25	$4,200,000	$5,700,000	
3.300	2062.06.18	S	BCCD-30	11070TAD0	BD	2013	$230,500	$230,500	

GUARANTEED DEBT
March 31, 2025

							Issued	Outstanding	Ref.
Cpn %	Maturity	Freq	Series	CUSIP	Type	Year	Amount (000)	Amount (000)	Note

BRITISH COLUMBIA INVESTMENT MANAGEMENT CORPORATION

3.400	2030.06.02	S	2	110610AC6	SN	'24-'25	$3,000,000	$3,000,000	
4.900	2033.06.02	S	1	110610AA0	NT	'23-'24	$2,250,000	$2,250,000	

REFERENCES
1. Callable if taxation laws requiring additional payments are imposed or levied.

Manitoba

Premier: Wab Kinew (New Democratic Party)
Capital City: Winnipeg
Area: 647,797 sq. kilometres

Visit this Web site:
Province of Manitoba: www.gov.mb.ca

DBRS Bond Rating at November 4, 2024 ... A high

		2024	2023
Employed		729,100	703,100
Unemployment rate (%)		6.2	4.2
Average weekly earnings (Dec.)		$1,142.96	$1,115.59
Building permits		$4,583,705,000	$3,887,563,000
Retail sales		$25,021,973,000	$26,958,089,000
Population (est. July 1)		1,494,301	1,454,902
December consumer price index (2002=100)		160	158.2
Sales tax	(GST)	5%	5%
	(PST)	7%	7%

DIRECT DEBT
March 31, 2025

						Issued		Outstanding	Ref.
Cpn %	Maturity	Freq	Series	CUSIP	Type	Year	Amount (000)	Amount (000)	Note
PROVINCE OF MANITOBA									
2.450	2025.06.02	S	GJ	563469UE3	DB	'15-'20	$2,950,000	$2,950,000	
4.800	2025.06.30	S	C086	56344ZLV9	MN	2006	$50,000	$50,000	1
4.400	2025.09.05	S	C119	56344ZPH6	DB	'10-'13	$715,000	$715,000	
7.750	2025.12.22	S	DT	563469DS1	DB	1995	$300,000	$300,000	2
0.200	2026.04.20	A			NT	2020	SFr100,000	SFr100,000	
2.550	2026.06.02	S	GN	563469UJ2	DB	'16-'17	$1,900,000	$1,900,000	
3.750	2026.06.09	S	C145		NT	'15-'16	A$290,000	A$290,000	
2.125	2026.06.22	S	GP	563469UL7	DB	2016	US$500,000	US$500,000	
2.600	2027.06.02	S	GS	563469UP8	DB	'17-'18	$1,500,000	$1,500,000	
3.600	2027.08.17	S	C157		MN	'17-'18	A$300,000	A$300,000	
3.000	2028.06.02	S		563469UR4	DB	'18-'23	$2,050,000	$2,050,000	
3.500	2028.08.22	S	C161		MN	'18-'19	A$225,000	A$225,000	
1.500	2028.10.25	S	HB	563469UY9	DB	2021	US$1,000,000	US$1,000,000	
2.570	2028.11.28	A	C155		MN	2016	HK$1,070,000	HK$1,070,000	
0.250	2029.03.15	A			NT	2019	SFr250,000	SFr250,000	
2.915	2029.04.10	S	C169		NT	2019	NZ$39,500	NZ$39,500	
2.750	2029.06.02	S		563469UT0	DB	'19-'23	$1,800,000	$1,800,000	
3.250	2029.09.05	S	C136	56344ZQC6	MN	'13-'16	$456,000	$456,000	
5.550	2029.12.03	S	C074	56344ZJD2	MN	2004	$100,000	$100,000	3
2.050	2030.06.02	S		563469UV5	DB	'20-'21	$1,300,000	$1,300,000	
10.500	2031.03.05	S	CL	563469CX1	DB	1990	$599,945	$599,945	4
6.300	2031.03.05	S	D025	56344ZCG2	MN	'00-'10	$410,000	$410,000	
4.875	2031.03.05	S	D129	56344ZKL2	MN	2005	$100,000	$100,000	5
2.050	2031.06.02	S		563469UX1	NT	'21-'22	$1,900,000	$1,900,000	
2.750	2032.02.03	S			MN	2022	A$36,000	A$36,000	
6.300	2032.07.26	S	C049	56344ZEH8	MN	2002	$50,000	$50,000	6
6.300	2032.10.29	S	C052	56344ZEW5	MN	2002	$30,000	$30,000	7
3.900	2032.12.02	S		563469VA0	NT	'22-'23	$1,650,000	$1,650,000	
2.850	2033.02.03	S			MN	2022	A$36,000	A$36,000	
3.800	2033.06.02	S		563469VB8	DB	'23-'24	$1,500,000	$1,500,000	
4.300	2033.07.27	S	HF	563469VC6	DB	2023	US$1,000,000	US$1,000,000	
3.750	2033.09.05	S	C141	56344ZQF9	MN	2014	$130,000	$130,000	
1.523	2034.05.16	A			NT	2024	SFr130,000	SFr130,000	
4.900	2034.05.31	S	HI	563469VF9	DB	2024	US$1,000,000	US$1,000,000	
4.250	2034.06.02	S		563469VE2	DB	'24-'25	$2,200,000	$2,200,000	
1.252	2034.07.18	A			MN	2019	SKr500,000	SKr500,000	
F.R.	2034.08.23	Q			NT	2024	€50,000	€50,000	
4.830	2034.08.28	S			NT	2024	A$600,000	A$600,000	
5.330	2035.01.19	S	C076	56344ZJM2	MN	2005	$75,000	$75,000	8
0.600	2035.03.30	A			MN	2020	€60,000	€60,000	
0.866	2035.04.16	A			MN	2025	SFr210,000	SFr210,000	
3.700	2035.06.02	S		563469VG7	DB	2025	$400,000	$900,000	
1.390	2035.06.11	A	C142		NT	2015	€32,000	€32,000	9
2.000	2036.12.01	S	C087	56344ZLW7	MN	2006	$100,000	$100,000	
0.750	2037.02.02	A			MN	2022	€70,000	€70,000	
3.740	2037.02.16	A			MN	2022	NZ$130,000	NZ$130,000	

FP Bonds — Government 2025

Cpn %	Maturity	Freq	Series	CUSIP	Type	Year	Issued Amount (000)	Outstanding Amount (000)	Ref. Note
5.700	2037.03.05	S	FA	563469EZ4	DB	'04-'06	$700,000	$700,000	
4.600	2038.03.05	S	PB	563469FL4	DB	2007	$950,000	$950,000	
4.250	2039.03.05	S	C124	56344ZPN3	MN	2011	$210,000	$210,000	
0.800	2039.03.15	A			MN	2019	SFr150,000	SFr150,000	
1.000	2039.06.25	A	C154		MN	2016	€40,000	€40,000	
4.650	2039.07.16	S	C091	56344ZME6	MN	2007	$100,000	$100,000	10
6.200	2040.03.05	S	C031	56344ZCK3	MN	'00-'01	$276,000	$276,000	
4.650	2040.03.05	S	FK	563469FQ3	DB	'08-'10	$800,000	$800,000	
0.700	2040.04.20	A			NT	2020	SFr100,000	SFr100,000	
1.770	2040.06.25	A	C143		NT	'15-'16	€470,000	€470,000	
1.740	2041.02.25	A	C147		NT	2016	€85,000	€85,000	
4.100	2041.03.05	S	FR	563469TM7	DB	'10-'15	$1,300,000	$1,300,000	
1.500	2041.06.25	A	C151		MN	'16-'19	€285,000	€285,000	
1.950	2041.06.25	A	H062		MN	2016	€45,000	€45,000	
0.700	2041.11.25	A			MN	2021	€160,000	€160,000	
6.000	2042.03.05	S	C040	56344ZDP1	MN	2002	$350,000	$350,000	
4.400	2042.03.05	S	FT	563469TQ8	DB	2011	$400,000	$400,000	
3.350	2043.03.05	S	GA	563469TW5	DB	'12-'13	$550,000	$550,000	
5.800	2044.03.05	S	C068	56344ZHN2	MN	'04-'06	$120,000	$120,000	
5.000	2044.09.05	S	C092	56344ZMF3	MN	'07-'11	$157,035	$157,035	
4.050	2045.09.05	S	GG	563469UB9	DB	'13-'14	$1,500,000	$1,500,000	
0.800	2046.04.27	S	C149		NT	2016	Jp¥5,000,000	Jp¥5,000,000	
0.700	2046.08.30	S	C153		MN	2016	Jp¥6,000,000	Jp¥6,000,000	
2.850	2046.09.05	S	GK	563469UF0	DB	'15-'16	$1,950,000	$1,950,000	
0.700	2046.12.05	S	C156		MN	2016	Jp¥5,000,000	Jp¥5,000,000	
3.400	2048.09.05	S	GR	563469UN3	DB	'17-'18	$2,100,000	$2,100,000	
1.500	2049.06.25	A	C170		NT	2019	€100,000	€100,000	
1.250	2049.06.25	A	C176		NT	2020	€75,000	€75,000	
0.475	2049.11.02	A			NT	2020	€100,000	€100,000	
4.700	2050.03.05	S	FN	563469TH8	DB	'09-'12	$350,000	$350,000	
3.200	2050.03.05	S	GV	563469US2	DB	'18-'20	$2,550,000	$2,550,000	
2.050	2052.09.05	S		563469UW3	DB	'20-'21	$1,800,000	$1,800,000	
3.150	2052.09.05	S	C129	56344ZPV5	MN	'12-'14	$610,000	$610,000	
3.800	2053.09.05	S		563469UZ6	DB	'22-'23	$1,900,000	$1,900,000	
3.650	2054.09.05	S	C139	56344ZQG7	MN	2014	$75,000	$75,000	
4.400	2055.09.05	S		563469VD4	NT	'24-'25	$2,300,000	$2,300,000	
5.200	2060.03.05	S	C110	56344ZNV7	MN	'09-'12	$325,000	$325,000	
4.625	2063.03.05	S	C109	56344ZNU9	MN	'09-'15	$255,000	$255,000	
3.450	2063.03.05	S	C137	56344ZQE2	MN	'13-'17	$1,199,000	$1,199,000	
3.100	2068.03.05	S	C160	56344ZQJ1	MN	'18-'24	$2,015,000	$2,015,000	
4.600	2074.03.05	S		56344ZQN2	MN	2024	$300,000	$300,000	
2.950	2120.09.05	S		56344ZQM4	MN	'20-'24	$650,000	$600,000	

REFERENCES

1. Extendible semiannually to June 30, 2036 at an interest rate of 4.8%.
2. Issued on behalf of Manitoba Hydro.
3. Extendible at the option of the holder to Dec. 3, 2029 with an interest rate of 5.55%.
4. Of the total, $299,945,000 issued on the exercise of warrants attached to the initial $300,000,000 issue.
5. Extendible to Mar. 5, 2031 with an interest rate of 4.875%.
6. Extendible to July 26, 2032 with an interest rate of 6.3%.
7. Extendible to Oct. 29, 2032 with an interest rate of 6.3%.

8. Extendible to Jan. 19, 2035 with an interest rate of 5.33%.
9. Redeem. at par in whole but not in part once on June 11, 2025 upon 5 business days' notice.
10. Puttable at par at the holder's option effective July 16, 2018.

New Brunswick

Premier: Susan Holt (Liberal)
Capital City: Fredericton
Area: 72,908 sq. kilometres

Visit this Web site:
   Province of New Brunswick: www.gnb.ca

DBRS Bond Rating at May 26, 2025 ... A high

	2024	2023
Employed	400,000	390,800
Unemployment rate (%)	7.7	6.3
Average weekly earnings (Dec.)	$1,182.22	$1,116.94
Building permits	$1,904,253,000	$1,741,251,000
Retail sales	$17,848,218,000	$17,224,115,000
Population (est. July 1)	854,355	834,691
December consumer price index (2002=100)	160.3	157.8
Sales tax (HST)	15%	15%

DIRECT DEBT
March 31, 2025

Cpn %	Maturity	Freq	Series	CUSIP	Type	Year	Issued Amount (000)	Outstanding Amount (000)	Ref. Note
PROVINCE OF NEW BRUNSWICK									
1.800	2025.08.14	S	IF	642866GR2	BD	'20-'22	$1,000,000	$1,000,000	
2.600	2026.08.14	S	HS	642866GK7	DB	'16-'21	$1,000,000	$1,000,000	
2.350	2027.08.14	S	HX	642866GM3	DB	'17-'18	$1,000,000	$1,000,000	
3.625	2028.05.15	S	HW	642869AM3	BD	2018	US$500,000	US$500,000	
3.100	2028.08.14	S	HZ	642866GN1	DB	'18-'22	$1,200,000	$1,200,000	
5.650	2028.12.27	S	FT	642866ET0	DB	'98-'99	$500,000	$500,000	
0.250	2029.01.19	A	HV		NT	'17-'18	SFr300,000	SFr300,000	
4.250	2029.08.14	S	IM	642866HD2	DB	2024	$500,000	$500,000	
6.290	2029.12.15	S	FV	642866EW3	DB	1999	$50,000	$50,000	1
2.550	2031.08.14	S	II	642866GT8	NT	2022	$600,000	$600,000	
0.200	2031.11.07	A	HU		NT	2016	SFr400,000	SFr400,000	
3.950	2032.08.14	S	IJ	642866HA8	DB	'22-'23	$1,200,000	$1,200,000	
0.125	2032.12.06	A	IE		NT	2019	SFr100,000	SFr100,000	
4.450	2033.08.14	S	IK	642866HB6	DB	'23-'24	$900,000	$900,000	
5.500	2034.01.27	S	GJ	642866FR3	DB	2004	$550,000	$550,000	
4.050	2034.08.14	S	IN	642866A98	NT	'24-'25	$900,000	$900,000	
4.650	2035.09.26	S	GO	642866FW2	DB	'05-'07	$650,000	$650,000	2
4.550	2037.03.26	S	GS	642866FZ5	DB	2007	$900,000	$900,000	2
4.800	2039.09.26	S	GT	642866GA9	DB	'07-'10	$1,200,000	$1,200,000	
0.250	2039.12.06	A	ID		NT	2019	SFr125,000	SFr125,000	
4.800	2041.06.03	S	HB	642869AA9	DB	'10-'14	$1,175,000	$1,175,000	
3.550	2043.06.03	S	HH	642869AE1	DB	'12-'14	$1,200,000	$1,200,000	
3.800	2045.08.14	S	HO	642866GG6	DB	'14-'15	$1,250,000	$1,250,000	
3.100	2048.08.14	S	HT	642866GL5	BD	'16-'18	$1,150,000	$1,150,000	
3.050	2050.08.14	S	IC	642866GQ4	DB	'19-'20	$1,500,000	$1,500,000	
2.900	2052.08.14	S	IH	642866GS0	DB	'21-'23	$600,000	$600,000	
5.000	2054.08.14	S	IL	642866HC4	NT	'23-'24	$900,000	$900,000	
3.550	2055.06.03	S	HG	642866GE1	NT	2012	$315,000	$315,000	
3.550	2065.06.03	S	HK	642866GF8	MN	'13-'19	$585,000	$585,000	

GUARANTEED DEBT
March 31, 2025

Cpn %	Maturity	Freq	Series	CUSIP	Type	Year	Issued Amount (000)	Outstanding Amount (000)	Ref. Note
NEW BRUNSWICK MUNICIPAL FINANCE CORPORATION									
Var.	2014.06.14-2033	S	BI		SB	2013	$73,647	$21,700	
Var.	2014.11.20-2033	S	BJ		SB	2013	$52,370	$12,943	
Var.	2015.05.15-2034	S	BK		SB	2014	$47,517	$9,844	
Var.	2015.12.08-2034	S	BL		SB	2014	$80,661	$24,540	

REFERENCES
1. Was puttable at par on Dec. 15, 2007 at the option of the noteholder. Prior to Dec. 15, 2007, the interest rate was 5.75%.

2. Proceeds from these issues split between Province of New Brunswick and New Brunswick Power; each pay 1.5% and 1%, respectively, on their share of the proceeds.

Newfoundland and Labrador

Premier: John Hogan (Liberal)
Capital City: St John's
Area: 405,212 sq. kilometres

Visit these Web sites:
    Province of Newfoundland and Labrador: www.gov.nf.ca
    Newfoundland and Labrador Hydro: nlhydro.com

DBRS Bond Rating at July 23, 2024 ... A

	2024	2023
Employed	243,200	238,000
Unemployment rate (%)	10.5	10.5
Average weekly earnings (Dec.)	$1,273.39	$1,229.55
Building permits	$659,909,000	$474,994,000
Retail sales	$12,147,697,000	$11,414,146,000
Population (est. July 1)	545,247	538,605
December consumer price index (2002=100)	160.7	159.8
Sales tax (HST)	15%	15%

DIRECT DEBT
March 31, 2025

Cpn %	Maturity	Freq	Series	CUSIP	Type	Year	Issued Amount (000)	Outstanding Amount (000)	Ref. Note
PROVINCE OF NEWFOUNDLAND AND LABRADOR									
2.300	2025.06.02	S	6W	651333FS0	DB	'15-'20	$1,050,000	$1,050,000	
9.150	2025.07.07	S	6B	651333EA0	DB	1995	$100,000	$100,000	
8.450	2026.02.05	S	6C	651333EB8	DB	1996	$150,000	$150,000	
3.000	2026.06.02	S	6Z	651333FV3	DB	2016	$1,000,000	$1,000,000	
1.250	2027.06.02	S	7J	651333GF7	DB	2020	$500,000	$500,000	
3.850	2027.10.17	S	7M	651333GK6	DB	'22-'23	$1,400,000	$1,400,000	
6.150	2028.04.17	S	6F	651333EE2	DB	1998	$450,000	$450,000	
2.850	2028.06.02	S	7D	651333FZ4	BD	'17-'22	$1,250,000	$1,250,000	
2.850	2029.06.02	S	7G	651333GC4	DB	'19-'20	$1,000,000	$1,000,000	
6.500	2029.10.17	S	6H	651333EG7	DB	1999	$200,000	$200,000	
1.750	2030.06.02	S	7I	651333GE0	DB	'20-'21	$1,000,000	$1,000,000	
6.550	2030.10.17	S	6K	651333EZ5	DB	2000	$450,000	$450,000	
2.050	2031.06.02	S	7K	651333GG5	DB	'21-'22	$900,000	$900,000	
4.150	2033.06.02	S	7O	651333GM2	DB	'23-'24	$900,000	$900,000	
5.600	2033.10.17	S	6R	651333FM3	DB	2003	$300,000	$300,000	
0.800	2033.12.19	A	E002		NT	2024	SFr100,000	SFr100,000	
3.850	2034.12.02	S	7Q	651333GP5	DB	'24-'25	$1,065,000	$1,065,000	
3.067	2034.12.04	A	E001		NT	2024	€50,000	€50,000	
5.700	2035.10.17	S	6T	651333FP6	DB	2004	$300,000	$300,000	
4.500	2037.04.17	S	6U	651333FQ4	DB	2006	$350,000	$350,000	
4.650	2040.10.17	S	6V	651333FR2	DB	2007	$650,000	$650,000	
6.240	2042.10.17	S	6Q	651333FK7	DB	2002	$250,000	$250,000	
3.300	2046.10.17	S	6X	651333FT8	DB	'15-'16	$2,050,000	$2,050,000	
3.700	2048.10.17	S	7C	651333FY7	DB	'16-'19	$1,350,000	$1,350,000	
2.650	2050.10.17	S	7H	651333GD2	DB	'19-'21	$1,900,000	$1,900,000	
3.150	2052.12.02	S	7L	651333GH3	DB	'21-'22	$750,000	$750,000	
4.100	2054.10.17	S	7N	651333GL4	DB	'22-'24	$1,500,000	$900,000	
4.600	2055.10.17	S		651333GN0	BD	2024	$900,000	$900,000	

GUARANTEED DEBT
March 31, 2025

Cpn %	Maturity	Freq	Series	CUSIP	Type	Year	Issued Amount (000)	Outstanding Amount (000)	Ref. Note
LABRADOR ISLAND LINK FUNDING TRUST									
3.760	2033.06.01	S	A	505443AA9	BD	2013	$725,000	$725,000	
3.860	2045.12.01	S	B	505443AB7	BD	2013	$600,000	$600,000	
3.850	2053.12.01	S	C	505443AC5	BD	2013	$1,075,000	$1,075,000	
Var.	2020.12.01-2057	S			SB	2017	$1,050,000	$955,500	

Cpn %	Maturity	Freq	Series	CUSIP	Type	Year	Issued Amount (000)	Outstanding Amount (000)	Ref. Note
MUSKRAT FALLS/LABRADOR TRANSMISSION ASSETS FUNDING TRUST									
3.630	2029.06.01	S	A	628153AA6	BD	2013	$650,000	$650,000	
3.830	2037.06.01	S	B	628153AB4	BD	2013	$675,000	$675,000	
3.860	2048.12.01	S	C	628153AC2	BD	2013	$1,275,000	$1,275,000	
Var.	2020.12.01-2052	S			SB	2017	$1,850,000	$1,666,349	
Var.	2037.12.01-2057				SB	2022	$1,000,000	$1,000,000	
NEWFOUNDLAND AND LABRADOR HYDRO									
8.400	2026.02.27	S	Y	651329AW4	DB	1996	$300,000	$300,000	
6.650	2031.08.27	S	AB	651329BA1	DB	'01-'02	$300,000	$300,000	
5.700	2033.07.14	S	AD	651329BC7	DB	2003	$125,000	$125,000	
3.600	2045.12.01	S	AF	651329BE3	DB	'14-'17	$500,000	$500,000	

Nova Scotia

Premier: Tim Houston (Progressive Conservative)
Capital City: Halifax
Area: 55,284 sq. kilometres

Visit this Web site:
   Province of Nova Scotia: www.novascotia.ca

DBRS Bond Rating at November 5, 2024 ... A high

	2024	2023
Employed	527,700	507,900
Unemployment rate (%)	6.3	5.9
Average weekly earnings (Dec.)	$1,139.45	$1,084.13
Building permits	$3,445,069,000	$2,883,618,000
Retail sales	$21,743,791,000	$21,205,457,000
Population (est. July 1)	1,076,374	1,058,694
December consumer price index (2002=100)	163.6	162.1
Sales tax (HST)	15%	15%

DIRECT DEBT
March 31, 2025

Cpn %	Maturity	Freq	Series	CUSIP	Type	Year	Issued Amount (000)	Outstanding Amount (000)	Ref. Note
PROVINCE OF NOVA SCOTIA									
1.350	2025.04.21	S	P126	66989ZEW4	NT	2020	$535,000	$535,000	
2.150	2025.06.01	S	D8	669827BG1	BD	2015	$300,000	$300,000	
6.600	2027.06.01	S	9Z	669827EB9	BD	'97-'98	$550,000	$550,000	
2.100	2027.06.01	S	D9	669827GA9	BD	2016	$650,000	$650,000	
1.100	2028.06.01	S	E3	669827GD3	BD	'21-'23	$1,100,000	$1,100,000	
F.R.	2029.05.09	Q	P127	669827GJ0	NT	2024	$500,000	$500,000	
4.050	2029.06.01	S	E5	669827GF8	DB	2023	$600,000	$600,000	
2.000	2030.09.01	S	E2	669827GC5	DB	'20-'21	$1,200,000	$1,200,000	
6.600	2031.12.01	S	B2	669827EW3	BD	2001	$300,000	$300,000	
2.400	2031.12.01	S	E4	669827GE1	BD	'21-'22	$900,000	$900,000	
F.R.	2032.06.01	Q		669827GL5	BD	2024	$500,000	$500,000	
5.800	2033.06.01	S	B5	669827FL6	BD	'03-'04	$600,000	$600,000	
4.050	2033.06.01	S	E6	669827GG6	DB	2023	$600,000	$600,000	
3.850	2035.06.01	S		669827GM3	DB	2024	$400,000	$400,000	
4.900	2035.06.01	S	B7	669827FP7	DB	2005	$350,000	$350,000	
4.500	2037.06.01	S	B8	669827FQ5	BD	'06-'08	$750,000	$750,000	
4.700	2041.06.01	S	D3	669827FW2	BD	'09-'10	$950,000	$950,000	
4.400	2042.06.01	S	D6	6698278Z3	DB	'11-'12	$1,050,000	$1,050,000	
3.450	2045.06.01	S	D7	669827FZ5	DB	'14-'15	$325,000	$325,000	
3.150	2051.12.01	S	E1	669827GB7	DB	'19-'21	$2,000,000	$2,000,000	
4.750	2054.12.01	S	E7	669827GH4	NT	'23-'24	$1,500,000	$1,500,000	
4.600	2055.12.01	S		669827A98	DB	2025	$400,000	$900,000	
3.500	2062.06.02	S	P112	66989ZEG9	MN	'12-'13	$1,488,800	$1,488,800	
4.750	2074.06.01	S		669827GK7	NT	2024	$300,000	$300,000	

GUARANTEED DEBT
March 31, 2025

Cpn %	Maturity	Freq	Series	CUSIP	Type	Year	Issued Amount (000)	Outstanding Amount (000)	Ref. Note
NOVA SCOTIA POWER FINANCE CORPORATION									
11.000	2031.02.26	S	AM	669812BP3	NT	1991	$200,000	$200,000	

Ontario

Premier: Doug Ford (Progressive Conservative)
Capital City: Toronto
Area: 1,076,395 sq. kilometres

Visit these Web sites:
　　Province of Ontario: www.ontario.ca
　　Ontario Electricity Financial Corporation: www.oefc.on.ca

DBRS Bond Rating at December 5, 2024 ... AA

	2024	2023
Employed	8,201,400	7,913,900
Unemployment rate (%)	7.5	6.3
Average weekly earnings (Dec.)	$1,331.34	$1,238.15
Building permits	$59,511,293,000	$56,188,581,000
Retail sales	$299,845,168,000	$297,331,543,000
Population (est. July 1)	16,124,116	15,608,369
December consumer price index (2002=100)	162.7	160
Sales tax (HST)	13%	13%

DIRECT DEBT
March 31, 2025

Cpn %	Maturity	Freq	Series	CUSIP	Type	Year	Issued Amount (000)	Outstanding Amount (000)	Ref. Note
PROVINCE OF ONTARIO									
0.625	2025.04.17	A	EMTN116		BD	2018	€1,500,000	€1,500,000	
2.600	2025.06.02	S	DMTN227	68323ACX0	BD	2015	$13,600,000	$13,600,000	1
9.500	2025.06.02	S	JE	683234JA7	BD	1994	$500,000	$460,000	
2.350	2025.06.21	A	15A	68323ADG6	SV	2015		$3,308	
2.350	2025.06.21		15C	68323ADD3	SV	2015		$2,616	2
3.100	2025.08.26	S	ADI4		BD	'15-'16	A$365,000	A$365,000	
1.750	2025.09.08	S	DMTN245	68333ZAK3	BD	2020	$9,050,000	$9,050,000	
8.500	2025.12.02	S	JQ	683234JQ2	BD	1995	$1,000,000	$1,000,000	
0.625	2026.01.21	S	G87	683234AS7	BD	2021	US$3,500,000	US$3,500,000	
8.000	2026.02.06	S	JY	683234JV1	BD	1996	$50,000	$12,500	
1.050	2026.04.14	S	G89	683234AT5	BD	2021	US$3,000,000	US$3,000,000	
2.500	2026.04.27	S	G69	68323ADP6	BD	2016	US$1,000,000	US$1,000,000	
2.250	2026.05.26	A	EMTN126		BD	2022	£500,000	£500,000	
2.400	2026.06.02	S	DMTN229	68323ADM3	BD	2016	$7,500,000	$7,500,000	
8.000	2026.06.02	S	JU	683234JT6	BD	'95-'96	$1,000,000	$1,000,000	
2.300	2026.06.15	S	G83	68323AFF6	BD	2019	US$1,750,000	US$1,750,000	
2.200	2026.06.21	A	16A	68323ADT8	SV	2016		$6,087	
2.200	2026.06.21		16C	68323ADU5	SV	2016		$4,945	2
1.350	2026.09.08	S	DMTN250	68333ZAQ0	BD	'21-'22	$2,000,000	$2,000,000	
8.000	2026.12.02	S	KR	683234KN7	BD	'97-'98	$425,000	$386,500	3
7.000	2026.12.02	S	MH	683234MK1	BD	1999	$124,584	$124,584	4
0.250	2026.12.15	A	EMTN121		BD	2021	£1,750,000	£1,750,000	
3.500	2027.01.27	S	ADI5		BD	2017	A$315,000	A$315,000	
1.850	2027.02.01	S	DMTN244	68333ZAJ6	BD	'20-'21	$3,250,000	$3,250,000	5
7.500	2027.02.03	S	KN	683234KJ6	BD	1997	$300,000	$58,220	
6.950	2027.02.03	S	KT	683234KQ0	MN	1997	$200,000	$8,726	
7.500	2027.02.03	S	KY	683234KS6	BD	1997	$68,000	$11,549	6
7.500	2027.02.03	S	LA	683234LA4	BD	1997	$50,000	$5,507	
7.375	2027.02.04	S	KQ	683234KM9	BD	1998	$125,000	$990	7
0.375	2027.04.08	A	EMTN117		BD	2020	€1,000,000	€1,000,000	
3.100	2027.05.19	S	G92	683234DB1	BD	2022	US$2,250,000	US$2,250,000	
1.050	2027.05.21	S	G85	683234AQ1	BD	2020	US$1,750,000	US$1,750,000	
2.600	2027.06.02	S	DMTN234	68323AEE0	BD	'17-'20	$8,400,000	$8,400,000	
7.600	2027.06.02	S	KJ	683234KG2	BD	'96-'04	$4,835,200	$4,835,200	1
2.150	2027.06.21	A	17A	68323AEN0	SV	2017		$4,073	
2.150	2027.06.21		17C	68323AEJ9	SV	2017		$2,679	2
1.050	2027.09.08	S	DMTN247	68333ZAM9	BD	2020	$2,000,000	$2,000,000	
3.600	2028.03.08	S	DMTN256	68333ZAW7	DB	'22-'23	$5,500,000	$5,500,000	
2.900	2028.06.02	S	DMTN238	68333ZAC1	BD	'18-'19	$9,550,000	$9,550,000	
2.850	2028.06.21	A	18A	68323AEZ3	SV	2018		$734	
2.850	2028.06.21		18C	68323AFA7	SV	2018		$1,075	2
6.250	2028.08.25	S	LQ	683234LN6	BD	'98-'99	$723,843	$80,620	1
3.400	2028.09.08	S	DMTN259	68333ZAZ0	DB	2023	$2,000,000	$2,000,000	
3.200	2028.10.12	S	ADI6		BD	'18-'21	A$115,000	A$115,000	
F.R.	2028.11.27	Q	DMTN261	68333ZBB2	BD	2023	$2,600,000	$2,600,000	
4.200	2029.01.18	S	G93	683234DQ8	BD	2024	US$3,000,000	US$3,000,000	

FP Bonds — Government 2025

Cpn %	Maturity	Freq	Series	CUSIP	Type	Year	Issued Amount (000)	Outstanding Amount (000)	Ref. Note
4.000	2029.03.08	S	DMTN264	68333ZBE6	BD	2024	$2,750,000	$2,750,000	
6.500	2029.03.08	S	LK	683234LJ5	BD	'98-'04	$4,727,000	$4,727,000	
2.700	2029.06.02	S	DMTN240	68333ZAE7	BD	'19-'20	$9,325,000	$9,325,000	
0.250	2029.06.28	A	EMTN115		BD	2017	SFr400,000	SFr400,000	
3.700	2029.09.17	S	G95	683234AW8	BD	2024	US$2,000,000	US$2,000,000	
2.000	2029.10.02	S	G84	68323AFG4	BD	2019	US$1,250,000	US$1,250,000	
2.700	2029.10.26	S	ADI7		MN	2019	A$40,000	A$40,000	
1.550	2029.11.01	S	DMTN251	68333ZAR8	MN	'21-'22	$5,500,000	$5,500,000	5
4.700	2030.01.15	S	G96	683234ET1	BD	2025	US$3,000,000	US$3,000,000	
F.R.	2030.02.21	Q	DMTN270	68333ZBL0	BD	2025	$1,500,000	$1,500,000	
2.050	2030.06.02	S	DMTN243	68333ZAH0	BD	2020	$11,650,000	$11,650,000	
2.950	2030.09.08	S	DMTN271	68333ZBM8	DB	2025	$1,500,000	$2,500,000	
1.125	2030.10.07	S	G86	683234AR9	BD	2020	US$1,250,000	US$1,250,000	
0.010	2030.11.25	A	EMTN120		BD	2020	€2,500,000	€2,500,000	
1.350	2030.12.02	S	DMTN248	68333ZAN7	BD	'20-'21	$7,000,000	$7,000,000	
9.500	2031.01.13	S	JN	683234JN9	BD	1995	$125,000	$125,000	
1.600	2031.02.25	S	G88	68323AFH2	BD	2021	US$1,500,000	US$1,500,000	
5.200	2031.06.02	S	DMTN206	68323AAB0	MN	2010	$133,300	$133,300	
2.150	2031.06.02	S	DMTN249	68333ZAP2	DB	2021	$8,850,000	$8,850,000	
6.200	2031.06.02	S	NF	683234NM6	BD	'00-'02	$3,000,000	$3,000,000	
0.250	2031.06.09	A	EMTN123		BD	2021	€1,000,000	€1,000,000	
1.800	2031.10.14	S	G90	68323AFJ8	BD	2021	US$1,000,000	US$1,000,000	
2.250	2031.12.02	S	DMTN253	68333ZAT4	BD	'21-'22	$6,350,000	$6,350,000	
2.500	2031.12.10	S	ADI9		BD	2021	A$36,000	A$36,000	
2.125	2032.01.21	S	G91	683234AU2	BD	2022	US$1,500,000	US$1,500,000	
4.050	2032.02.02	S	DMTN257	68333ZAX5	BD	2023	$3,000,000	$3,000,000	5
3.750	2032.06.02	S	DMTN254	68333ZAU1	BD	'22-'23	$9,650,000	$9,650,000	
2.600	2032.12.10	S	ADI10		BD	2021	A$36,000	A$36,000	
4.100	2033.03.04	S	DMTN263	68333ZBD8	BD	2024	$2,750,000	$2,750,000	8
5.850	2033.03.08	S	DMTN110	683234VA3	MN	2004	$200,000	$188,000	9
5.850	2033.03.08	S	DMTN116	683234VP0	MN	2004	$100,000	$100,000	10
5.850	2033.03.08	S	DMTN61	683234SL3	BD	'03-'12	$4,674,610	$4,674,610	11
0.050	2033.05.12	A	EMTN122		BD	2021	SFr250,000	SFr250,000	
3.650	2033.06.02	S	DMTN258	68333ZAY3	BD	'23-'24	$12,950,000	$12,950,000	
3.100	2034.01.31	A	EMTN127		BD	2024	€1,250,000	€1,250,000	
3.650	2034.02.03	S	DMTN268	68333ZBJ5	BD	2025	$1,250,000	$1,250,000	8
5.050	2034.04.24	S	G94	683234AV0	BD	2024	US$1,500,000	US$1,500,000	
5.350	2034.05.08	S	ADI11		BD	2024	A$1,500,000	A$1,500,000	
4.150	2034.06.02	S	DMTN262	68333ZBC0	DB	2024	$12,250,000	$12,250,000	
5.000	2034.07.13	S	DMTN157	683234XT0	MN	2005	$47,500	$47,500	
9.400	2034.07.13	S	EMTN5		MN	1994	$300,000	$300,000	
2.000	2034.10.03	S	ADI8		NT	'19-'23	A$355,000	A$355,000	
9.750	2034.11.03	S	HY	683234HS0	BD	1994	$280,000	$248,800	
3.800	2034.12.02	S	DMTN266	68333ZBG1	BD	'24-'25	$7,500,000	$7,500,000	
Z.R.	2035.01.10		HZ-JD	683234HV3	BD	1994	$230,800	$21,049	12
9.500	2035.01.12	S	JG	683234JC3	BD	2007	$132,950	$110,950	13
9.875	2035.02.08	S	JJ	683234HU5	BD	1995	$73,000	$32,000	
5.600	2035.06.02	S	DMTN119	683234VR6	DB	'04-'16	$7,556,209	$7,338,509	14
5.350	2035.06.02	S	DMTN133	683234WK0	MN	2005	$150,000	$150,000	15
3.600	2035.06.02	S	DMTN269	68333ZBK2	DB	2025	$2,500,000	$6,250,000	
8.250	2036.06.20	S	KC	683234KC1	BD	1996	$211,000	$98,984	

Provinces

FP Bonds — Government 2025

Cpn %	Maturity	Freq	Series	CUSIP	Type	Year	Issued Amount (000)	Outstanding Amount (000)	Ref. Note
2.000	2036.12.01	S	DMTN158	683234XU7	BD	'05-'09	$2,844,000	$2,844,000	1,16
4.700	2037.06.02	S	DMTN164	683234YD4	MN	'06-'07	$9,100,000	$9,100,000	1
5.200	2037.12.20	S	DMTN138	683234WR5	MN	2005	$100,000	$100,000	
10.000	2038.06.02	S	DMTN117	683234VQ8	MN	2004	$75,000	$75,000	
8.100	2038.06.20	S	KG	683234KE7	BD	1996	$120,000	$120,000	
5.750	2038.07.13	S	LS	683234LW6	BD	1998	$50,000	$50,000	
6.000	2038.08.25	S	LT	683234LX4	BD	1998	$100,000	$86,500	
4.600	2039.06.02	S	DMTN182	683234ZP6	MN	'08-'10	$9,700,000	$9,700,000	1
5.650	2039.07.13	S	MK	683234MM7	BD	'99-'01	$300,000	$223,858	
5.700	2039.12.02	S	NE	683234NL8	BD	'00-'06	$1,489,000	$1,489,000	
6.200	2040.04.18	S	DMTN44	683234RF7	MN	'02-'05	$100,000	$100,000	
0.699	2040.10.02	A	EMTN118		BD	2020	€50,000	€50,000	
4.650	2041.06.02	S	DMTN204	683234B98	MN	'10-'11	$11,650,000	$11,650,000	1
1.820	2041.06.28	A	EMTN112		NT	2016	€52,000	€52,000	
6.200	2041.12.02	S	DMTN10	683234PS1	MN	'01-'06	$340,000	$340,000	
0.700	2041.12.09	A	EMTN125		BD	2021	€75,000	€75,000	
6.000	2042.03.08	S	DMTN29	683234QM3	MN	2001	$41,000	$41,000	
6.000	2042.06.02	S	DMTN33	683234QT8	MN	'02-'04	$240,000	$240,000	
3.500	2043.06.02	S	DMTN214	68323AAY0	MN	'12-'13	$11,200,000	$11,200,000	1
5.750	2043.06.02	S	DMTN62	683234SM1	MN	'03-'06	$75,000	$75,000	
4.600	2044.06.02	S	DMTN169	683234YR3	MN	2006	$27,000	$27,000	
Z.R.	2045.01.10		JL	683234JL3	BD	1995	$35,531	$35,531	17
9.500	2045.03.01	S	JK	683234JK5	BD	1995	$150,000	$150,000	18
4.500	2045.06.02	S	DMTN153	683234XP8	MN	'05-'06	$175,000	$175,000	
3.450	2045.06.02	S	DMTN220	68323ACC6	MN	'13-'14	$16,050,000	$16,050,000	1
4.850	2046.06.02	S	DMTN166	683234YN2	MN	'06-'07	$154,700	$154,700	
2.900	2046.12.02	S	DMTN228	68323ACY8	BD	'15-'16	$14,700,000	$14,700,000	1
0.760	2046.12.03	A	EMTN124		BD	2021	€160,000	€160,000	
4.500	2047.06.02	S	DMTN176	683234ZA9	MN	'07-'08	$158,000	$158,000	
4.700	2048.06.02	S	DMTN184	683234ZY7	MN	'08-'09	$50,000	$50,000	
2.800	2048.06.02	S	DMTN231	68323ADZ4	BD	'16-'17	$12,700,000	$12,700,000	
2.900	2049.06.02	S	DMTN236	68333ZAA5	BD	'17-'19	$13,250,000	$13,250,000	
2.650	2050.12.02	S	DMTN242	68333ZAG2	BD	'19-'20	$14,100,000	$14,100,000	
1.900	2051.12.02	S	DMTN246	68333ZAL1	BD	'20-'21	$12,750,000	$12,750,000	
2.550	2052.12.02	S	DMTN252	68333ZAS6	BD	'21-'22	$8,250,000	$8,250,000	
3.750	2053.12.02	S	DMTN255	68333ZAV9	BD	'22-'23	$12,400,000	$12,400,000	
4.600	2054.06.02	S	DMTN185	683234A24	MN	'08-'11	$40,000	$40,000	
4.100	2054.10.07	S	DMTN267	68333ZBH9	BD	2024	$1,000,000	$1,000,000	8
4.150	2054.12.02	S	DMTN260	68333ZBA4	NT	'23-'24	$12,000,000	$12,000,000	
4.600	2055.12.02	S	DMTN265	68333ZBF3	NT	'24-'25	$9,900,000	$12,250,000	
3.250	2062.06.02	S	DMTN216	68323ABP8	MN	'12-'23	$525,000	$525,000	

GUARANTEED DEBT
March 31, 2025

							Issued	Outstanding	Ref.
Cpn %	Maturity	Freq	Series	CUSIP	Type	Year	Amount (000)	Amount (000)	Note
OMERS FINANCE TRUST									
0.450	2025.05.13	A			NT	2020	€1,000,000	€1,000,000	
1.100	2026.03.26	S		682142AF1	NT	2021	US$1,000,000	US$1,000,000	
1.550	2027.04.21	S	B	682142AE4	NT	2020	$1,250,000	$1,250,000	
4.000	2028.04.20	S		682142AJ3	SN	2023	US$1,000,000	US$1,000,000	
3.125	2029.01.25	A			SN	2024	€750,000	€750,000	
2.600	2029.05.14	S	A	682142AC8	SN	2019	$1,000,000	$1,000,000	
4.500	2029.10.16	S			NT	2024	A$750,000	A$750,000	
4.375	2030.03.20	S		68218UAA6	SN	2025	US$1,000,000	US$1,000,000	
4.750	2031.03.26	S		682142AL8	NT	2024	US$1,000,000	US$1,000,000	
3.500	2032.04.19	S		682142AG9	NT	2022	US$600,000	US$600,000	
5.500	2033.11.15	S		682142AK0	NT	2023	US$1,000,000	US$1,000,000	
3.250	2035.01.28	A			SN	2025	€1,000,000	€1,000,000	
4.000	2052.04.19	S		682142AH7	NT	2022	US$500,000	US$500,000	
ONTARIO ELECTRICITY FINANCIAL CORPORATION									
8.500	2025.05.26	S	HYD-GB9	683078GB9	BD	1995	$500,000	$500,000	
9.000	2025.05.26	S	HYD-GD5	683078GD5	BD	1995	$500,000	$500,000	
8.250	2026.06.22	S	HYD-GG8	683078GG8	BD	1996	$1,000,000	$1,000,000	
6.594	2027.07.18	S	HYD-GR4	683078GR4	BD	1998	$114,900	$12,070	19
10.800	2031.04.11		HYD-FP9		BD	1991	$750,000	$750,000	20
6.000	2031.10.17	S	HYD-GT0-1	683078GT0	MN	1998	$100,000	$100,000	
ONTARIO TEACHERS' FINANCE TRUST									
1.375	2025.04.15	S		68329AAD0	SN	2020	US$1,000,000	US$1,000,000	
0.500	2025.05.06	A			SN	2020	€1,500,000	€1,500,000	
1.125	2026.05.15	A			NT	2021	£500,000	£500,000	
0.875	2026.09.21	S		68329AAK4	NT	2021	US$2,000,000	US$2,000,000	
3.000	2027.04.13	S	7	68329AAL2	NT	2022	US$1,500,000	US$1,500,000	
1.100	2027.10.19	S		68329AAE8	SN	2020	$1,250,000	$1,250,000	
4.250	2028.04.25	S	12	68329AAP3	SN	2023	US$1,500,000	US$1,500,000	
0.100	2028.05.19	A			MN	2021	€1,250,000	€1,250,000	
4.625	2029.04.10	S		68329AAQ1	NT	2024	US$1,500,000	US$1,500,000	
3.300	2029.10.05	A			SN	2022	€500,000	€500,000	
4.150	2029.11.01	S	11	C69798AW3	SN	2023	$1,000,000	$1,000,000	
1.250	2030.09.27	S		68329AAH1	SN	2020	US$1,500,000	US$1,500,000	
0.050	2030.11.25	A			BD	2020	€750,000	€750,000	
2.000	2031.04.16	S		68329AAJ7	NT	2021	US$1,500,000	US$1,500,000	
1.850	2032.05.03	A			MN	2022	€1,250,000	€1,250,000	
4.450	2032.06.02	S		68329AAM0	SN	2022	$1,000,000	$1,000,000	
4.300	2034.06.02	S		C69798AZ6	SN	2024	$1,000,000	$1,000,000	
0.900	2041.05.20	A			MN	2021	€1,250,000	€1,250,000	
0.950	2051.11.24	A			MN	2021	€500,000	€500,000	

CALLABLE BONDS
March 31, 2025

Coupon Rate %	Maturity Date	Next Call Date	Next Call Price	Call Flag
OMERS FINANCE TRUST				
4.000	2052.04.19	2051.10.19	US$100.00	C

REFERENCES
1. All or some of the amount issued is on-lent to Ontario Electricity Financial Corporation.
2. Interest is compounded and payable at maturity or, if redeemable, upon redemption.
3. An additional $200,000,000 of series KR bonds were issued on Sept. 29, 1998 upon exchange of a similar amount of series LF bonds.
4. The terms of these debentures require that a one-time interest payment of $31.1 million be made at maturity.
5. Green bonds.
6. Issued on Apr. 27, 1998 upon exchange of equal aggregate amount of 7.5% bonds due 2007.
7. Issued on Feb. 4, 1998 upon exchange of equal aggregate amount of 6.05% bonds due Feb. 4, 2002.
8. Green bonds issued under the Province's Sustainable Bond Framework.
9. Was retractable on Mar. 8, 2012 at par.
10. Extendible to Sept. 8, 2033 with an interest rate of 5.8%.
11. An additional $162,610,000 of series DMTN61 bonds were issued on Mar. 8, 2009 upon exchange of a similar amount of series DMTN102 bonds.
12. Zero coupon bonds which require unequal payments consisting of principal and interest to be made at predetermined irregular intervals. During the fiscal year 2010-11, principal repaid was $0.7 million. By Jan. 10, 2035, the principal to be repaid on these bonds will be $230,000,000.
13. Issued upon extension of equal aggregate amount of 9.5% bonds due Jan. 12, 2007.
14. Issued on Oct. 16, 2006 an additional $100,000,000 principal amount upon exchange of an equal amount of 5.6% bonds, series DMTN168, due June 2, 2035.
15. Was retractable on Dec. 2, 2014 at par. Previously, interest rate was 4.0%
16. Real return bonds.
17. The terms of these debentures require unequal payments, consisting of both principal and interest, to be made at predetermined irregular intervals with the final payment on Jan. 10, 2045. The total principal and interest to be payable over the life of the debenture is $1,325,000,000.
18. Was retractable on Mar. 1, 2010 at par.
19. Issued upon exchange of an equal amount of 5.682% bonds due July 18, 2003.
20. The annual coupons were stripped and the principal amount was restructured as a discount note which will mature at par.

Prince Edward Island

Premier: Rob Lantz (Progressive Conservative)
Capital City: Charlottetown
Area: 5,660 sq. kilometres

Visit this Web site:
  Province of Prince Edward Island: www.gov.pe.ca

DBRS Bond Rating at June 28, 2024 ... A

	2024	2023
Employed	94,600	91,900
Unemployment rate (%)	8.5	8.1
Average weekly earnings (Dec.)	$1,094.04	$1,022.91
Building permits	$796,058,000	$534,531,000
Retail sales	$3,568,100,000	$3,564,352,000
Population (est. July 1)	178,550	173,787
December consumer price index (2002=100)	163.6	163

DIRECT DEBT
March 31, 2025

Cpn %	Maturity	Freq	Series	CUSIP	Type	Year	Issued Amount (000)	Outstanding Amount (000)	Ref. Note
PROVINCE OF PRINCE EDWARD ISLAND									
2.350	2025.08.25	S		741666DA6	DB	2015	$125,000	$125,000	
6.100	2027.07.29	S		741666CN9	DB	2002	$100,000	$100,000	
1.200	2028.02.11	S		741666DC2	DB	2021	$125,000	$125,000	
6.800	2030.02.21	S		741666CL3	DB	2000	$80,000	$80,000	
1.850	2031.07.27	S		741666DD0	DB	'21-'22	$200,000	$200,000	
6.250	2032.01.29	S		741666CM1	DB	2002	$100,000	$100,000	
3.750	2032.12.01	S		741666DE8	DB	2023	$200,000	$200,000	
5.600	2034.02.21	S		741666CP4	DB	2003	$100,000	$100,000	
4.050	2034.06.02	S		741666DF5	DB	2024	$400,000	$400,000	
5.700	2035.06.15	S		741666CQ2	DB	2004	$100,000	$100,000	
3.950	2035.06.15	S		741666DG3	DB	2025	$200,000	$200,000	
5.300	2036.05.19	S		741666CR0	DB	2005	$100,000	$100,000	
4.650	2037.11.19	S		741666CS8	DB	'05-'10	$200,000	$200,000	
4.600	2041.05.19	S		741666CW9	DB	2011	$200,000	$200,000	
3.650	2042.06.27	S		741666CX7	DB	2012	$200,000	$200,000	
2.650	2051.12.01	S		741666DB4	DB	'19-'20	$225,000	$225,000	
3.600	2053.01.17	S		741666CY5	BD	'13-'14	$325,000	$325,000	
3.850	2054.07.17	S		741666CZ2	DB	2014	$125,000	$125,000	

GUARANTEED DEBT
March 31, 2025

Cpn %	Maturity	Freq	Series	CUSIP	Type	Year	Issued Amount (000)	Outstanding Amount (000)	Ref. Note
ISLAND WASTE MANAGEMENT CORPORATION									
6.400	2027.12.31	Q		464580AA7	NT	2002	$30,130	$6,003	

Québec

Premier: Francois Legault (Coalition Avenir Québec)
Capital City: Québec City
Area: 1,542,056 sq. kilometres

Visit these Web sites:
    Province of Québec: www.gouv.qc.ca
    CDP Financial Inc.: www.lacaisse.com
    Hydro-Québec: www.hydroquebec.com

DBRS Bond Rating at June 10, 2024 ... AA low

	2024	2023
Employed	4,619,900	4,531,900
Unemployment rate (%)	5.6	4.7
Average weekly earnings (Dec.)	$1,241.34	$1,167.1
Building permits	$27,576,692,000	$25,182,247,000
Retail sales	$180,303,418,000	$177,698,376,000
Population (est. July 1)	9,056,044	8,874,683
December consumer price index (2002=100)	157.5	155
Sales tax (GST)	5%	5%
(PST)	10%	10%

FP Bonds — Government 2025

DIRECT DEBT
March 31, 2025

Cpn %	Maturity	Freq	Series	CUSIP	Type	Year	Issued Amount (000)	Outstanding Amount (000)	Ref. Note
PROVINCE OF QUÉBEC									
0.200	2025.04.07	A	E210		BD	2020	€1,600,000	€1,600,000	
5.350	2025.06.01	S	B076	74814ZDE0	MN	'04-'07	$652,000	$652,000	
2.600	2025.07.06	S	QU	748148RX3	BD	2018	$500,000	$500,000	1
0.600	2025.07.23	S	RA	748148SC8	NT	2020	US$3,250,000	US$3,250,000	
2.750	2025.09.01	S	B116	74814ZEV1	MN	'15-'20	$7,200,000	$7,200,000	
1.125	2025.10.28	A	E198		MN	2015	€1,100,000	€1,100,000	
6.350	2026.01.30	S	49	74815HBZ4	MN	1996	US$150,000	US$149,875	2
7.140	2026.02.27	S	51	74815HCB6	MN	1996	US$100,000	US$99,770	3
7.485	2026.03.02	S		74815HCA8	MN	1996	US$150,000	US$150,000	
6.290	2026.03.06	S	52	74815HCC4	MN	1996	US$100,000	US$99,850	
7.035	2026.03.10	S	53	74815HCD2	MN	1996	US$50,000	US$50,000	4
8.500	2026.04.01	S	B033	74814ZBH5	MN	1996	$100,000	$100,000	
8.500	2026.04.01	S	B049	74814ZCA9	MN	1999	$90,000	$90,000	
7.500	2026.04.01	S	B067	74814ZDS9	MN	2002	$170,000	$165,850	5
5.500	2026.04.01	S	B070	74814ZCX9	MN	2003	$75,000	$74,332	
6.400	2026.04.01	S	B071	74814ZCY7	MN	2003	$90,000	$90,000	6
8.500	2026.04.01	S	OC	748148PZ0	BD	'96-'00	$2,176,100	$2,176,100	
7.380	2026.04.09	S	54	74815HCE0	MN	1996	US$100,000	US$100,000	
7.500	2026.04.15	S	55	74815HCF7	MN	1996	US$50,000	US$50,000	
7.500	2026.04.15	S	56	74815HCG5	MN	1996	US$50,000	US$50,000	7
2.500	2026.04.20	S	QP	748149AJ0	NT	2016	US$2,000,000	US$2,000,000	
3.700	2026.05.20	S	D007		MN	'15-'16	A$560,000	A$560,000	
7.295	2026.07.22	S	58	74815HCJ9	MN	1996	US$100,000	US$99,835	8
2.500	2026.09.01	S	B118	74814ZEX7	MN	2016	$6,000,000	$6,000,000	
2.250	2026.09.15	A	E215		MN	2022	£750,000	£750,000	
8.625	2026.12.01	S	KL	748148KA0	BD	1986	US$300,000	US$300,000	
4.500	2026.12.01	S	OP	748148QG1	BD	'98-'08	$859,920	$859,920	9
1.850	2027.02.13	S	QY	748148SA2	NT	2020	$500,000	$500,000	1
2.750	2027.04.12	S	QS	748149AN1	NT	2017	US$1,250,000	US$1,250,000	
0.875	2027.05.04	A	E200		MN	2017	€2,250,000	€2,250,000	
2.750	2027.09.01	S	B122	74814ZFB4	MN	'17-'18	$6,000,000	$6,000,000	
1.797	2028.01.01	Q	B092	74814ZDV2	MN	2008	$538,006	$90,453	
1.305	2028.03.21	S	E192		MN	2013	Jp¥5,000,000	Jp¥5,000,000	
6.100	2028.04.01	S		74814ZCD3	MN	1999	$5,000	$5,000	
3.625	2028.04.13	S	RC	748148SD6	NT	2023	US$3,500,000	US$3,500,000	
0.875	2028.07.05	A	E203		MN	2018	€1,000,000	€1,000,000	
2.750	2028.09.01	S	B124	74814ZFD0	MN	'18-'19	$6,000,000	$6,000,000	
3.250	2028.10.18	S	D008		MN	2018	A$160,000	A$160,000	
2.730	2029.04.03	S	E187		MN	2009	Jp¥13,000,000	Jp¥13,000,000	
4.500	2029.04.03	S	RE	748148M91	NT	2024	US$3,750,000	US$3,750,000	
2.854	2029.04.10	S	E206		MN	2019	NZ$66,000	NZ$66,000	
1.169	2029.04.11	A	E207		MN	2019	SKr1,700,000	SKr1,700,000	
2.900	2029.04.27	S	E189		MN	2009	Jp¥3,000,000	Jp¥3,000,000	
2.300	2029.09.01	S	B126	74814ZFF5	MN	'19-'20	$6,500,000	$6,500,000	
7.500	2029.09.15	S	PD	748148QR7	BD	1999	US$1,500,000	US$1,500,000	
6.000	2029.10.01	S	OS	748148QJ5	BD	'98-'02	$2,737,300	$2,737,300	

FP Bonds — Government 2025

Cpn %	Maturity	Freq	Series	CUSIP	Type	Year	Issued Amount (000)	Outstanding Amount (000)	Ref. Note
Z.R.	2029.10.15	A	E209		MN	2019	€1,000,000	€1,000,000	
2.600	2029.10.18	S	D009		MN	2019	A$100,000	A$100,000	
4.750	2030.01.22	A	E221		NT	2025	£750,000	£750,000	
4.140	2030.03.12	A	QH		BD	2010	€75,000	€75,000	
4.020	2030.04.29	A	QI		BD	2010	€35,000	€35,000	
1.350	2030.05.28	S	QZ	748148SB0	NT	2020	US$1,500,000	US$1,500,000	
1.900	2030.09.01	S	B127	74814ZFG3	MN	2020	$10,800,000	$10,800,000	
Z.R.	2030.10.29	A	E211		NT	2020	€2,250,000	€2,250,000	
1.900	2031.04.21	S	RB	748149AR2	NT	2021	US$1,000,000	US$1,000,000	
0.250	2031.05.05	A	E212		MN	2021	€2,500,000	€2,500,000	
2.100	2031.05.27	S	B130	74814ZFM0	NT	2021	$500,000	$500,000	1
0.030	2031.06.18	A	E213		NT	2021	SFr250,000	SFr250,000	
1.500	2031.09.01	S	B128	74814ZFH1	BD	'21-'22	$9,000,000	$9,000,000	
4.250	2031.12.01	S	PM	748148QZ9	BD	'01-'08	$947,880	$947,880	9
3.441	2031.12.01	S	PS	748148RF2	BD	2002	$97,000	$14,157	9
3.500	2031.12.15	A	QL		MN	2011	€27,000	€27,000	
0.500	2032.01.25	A	E214		BD	2022	€2,250,000	€2,250,000	
3.650	2032.05.20	S	B132	74814ZFP3	BD	2022	$1,000,000	$1,000,000	1
6.250	2032.06.01	S	PH	748148QT3	BD	'00-'03	$4,200,200	$4,200,200	
3.250	2032.09.01	S	B131	74814ZFN8	MN	'22-'23	$8,400,000	$8,400,000	
3.900	2032.11.22	S	B134	74814ZFR9	MN	'22-'23	$1,400,000	$1,400,000	1
3.000	2033.01.24	A	E216		NT	2023	€2,250,000	€2,250,000	
3.650	2033.04.06	S	D010		MN	2022	A$60,000	A$60,000	
2.040	2033.05.09	A	E217		NT	2023	SFr390,000	SFr390,000	
3.600	2033.09.01	S	B135	74814ZFS7	MN	'23-'24	$12,300,000	$12,300,000	
4.500	2033.09.08	S	RD	748148SE4	NT	2023	US$1,500,000	US$1,500,000	
3.125	2034.03.27	A	E218		MN	2024	€2,250,000	€2,250,000	
1.367	2034.04.26	A	E219		NT	2024	SFr290,000	SFr290,000	
5.250	2034.05.02	S	D011		MN	2024	A$1,350,000	A$1,350,000	
4.450	2034.09.01	S	B136	74814ZFT5	MN	'24-'25	$11,250,000	$12,000,000	
4.250	2034.09.05	S	RF	748148SF1	NT	2024	US$2,000,000	US$2,000,000	
6.500	2035.04.01	S		74814ZBP7	MN	1997	$300,000	$300,000	
Z.R.	2035.04.01			74814ZCB7	MN	1999	$456,000	$456,000	
Z.R.	2035.04.01		B009	74814ZAH6	MN	1995	$150,000	$150,000	10
V.R.	2035.04.01		B018	74814ZAS2	MN	1995	$150,000	$150,000	10
V.R.	2035.04.01		B019	74814ZAT0	MN	1995	$100,000	$100,000	10
5.400	2035.11.17	S	A063	74815HCP5	MN	2005	US$75,000	US$75,000	
7.970	2036.07.22	S	57	748148QH9	MN	1996	US$160,000	US$160,000	11
3.250	2036.12.01	S	B093	74814ZDW0	BD	'08-'10	$724,205	$724,205	9
5.750	2036.12.01	S	PX	748148RL9	BD	'03-'06	$4,082,900	$4,082,900	
5.000	2038.12.01	S	B082	74814ZDK6	MN	'06-'09	$5,000,000	$5,000,000	
3.350	2039.07.23	A	E220		NT	2024	€1,250,000	€1,250,000	
Z.R.	2039.10.01			74814ZCC5	MN	1999	$525,000	$525,000	
V.R.	2040.04.01		B057	74814ZCJ0	MN	'00-'01	$463,000	$463,000	10
5.000	2041.12.01	S	B102	74814ZEF6	MN	'09-'15	$9,200,000	$9,200,000	
5.600	2043.07.08	S	B069	74814ZCW1	MN	2003	$80,000	$80,000	
4.250	2043.12.01	S	B106	74814ZEK5	MN	'11-'17	$7,500,000	$7,500,000	
3.500	2045.12.01	S	B112	74814ZER0	MN	'13-'15	$10,000,000	$10,000,000	
3.500	2048.12.01	S	B117	74814ZEW9	MN	'15-'20	$11,650,000	$11,650,000	
5.100	2049.09.21	S	B094	74814ZDX8	MN	'08-'09	$13,440	$13,440	
5.000	2051.09.21	S	B085	74814ZDN0	MN	2006	$420,000	$420,000	

Provinces

FP Bonds — Government 2025

Cpn %	Maturity	Freq	Series	CUSIP	Type	Year	Issued Amount (000)	Outstanding Amount (000)	Ref. Note
3.100	2051.12.01	S	B125	74814ZFE8	MN	'19-'21	$14,000,000	$14,000,000	
5.100	2053.09.21	S	B095	74814ZDY6	MN	'08-'09	$37,192	$37,192	
2.850	2053.12.01	S	B129	74814ZFL2	MN	'21-'22	$11,500,000	$11,500,000	
4.400	2055.12.01	S	B133	74814ZFQ1	MN	'22-'24	$16,700,000	$16,700,000	
Z.R.	2056.12.01		B081	74814ZDJ9	MN	2006	$1,500,000	$1,500,000	
5.100	2057.09.21	S	B096	74814ZDZ3	MN	2008	$9,857	$9,857	
4.200	2057.12.01	S	B137	74814ZU27	NT	'24-'25	$4,200,000	$5,700,000	
5.100	2058.09.21	S	B097	74814ZEA7	MN	'08-'09	$38,326	$38,326	
5.100	2059.09.21	S	B098	74814ZEB5	MN	2008	$6,294	$6,294	
5.000	2061.09.21	S	B099	74814ZEC3	MN	2009	$25,000	$25,000	
6.700	2062.09.21	S	B086	74814ZDP5	MN	2006	$150,000	$150,000	
Z.R.	2065.06.01		B100	74814ZED1	MN	2009	$385,000	$385,000	
Z.R.	2065.06.01		B108	74814ZEM1	MN	2012	$335,000	$335,000	
6.350	2065.09.21	S	B084	74814ZDM2	MN	'06-'08	$940,000	$940,000	
Z.R.	2075.06.01		B109	74814ZEN9	MN	2012	$100,000	$100,000	
Z.R.	2076.12.01		B090	74814ZDT7	MN	2007	$500,000	$500,000	

GUARANTEED DEBT
March 31, 2025

Cpn %	Maturity	Freq	Series	CUSIP	Type	Year	Issued Amount (000)	Outstanding Amount (000)	Ref. Note
CDP FINANCIAL INC.									
F.R.	2025.05.19	Q		125094BD3	NT	2023	US$500,000	US$500,000	
0.875	2025.06.10			125094AU6	BD	2020	US$2,500,000	US$2,500,000	
4.500	2026.02.13	S	11	125094BB7	SN	2023	US$2,000,000	US$2,000,000	
1.000	2026.05.26	S	5	125094AV4	NT	2021	US$1,000,000	US$1,000,000	
1.500	2026.10.19	S		125094AW2	SN	2021	$1,250,000	$1,250,000	
1.750	2027.02.01	S	7	125094AX0	SN	2022	US$1,500,000	US$1,500,000	
1.125	2027.04.06	A			NT	2022	€2,000,000	€2,000,000	
3.800	2027.06.02	S		125094BA9	SN	2022	$1,250,000	$1,250,000	
3.700	2028.03.08	S		125094BC5	SN	2023	$2,000,000	$2,000,000	
4.250	2028.07.25	S	16	125094BE1	SN	2023	US$1,500,000	US$1,500,000	
3.000	2029.04.11	A			NT	2024	€1,500,000	€1,500,000	
4.875	2029.06.05	S		125094BG6	MN	2024	US$1,500,000	US$1,500,000	
3.950	2029.09.01	S		125094AZ5	SN	2022	$1,500,000	$1,500,000	
4.625	2030.01.24	S			NT	2025	US$1,500,000	US$1,500,000	
4.376	2030.05.15	S			SN	2023	A$300,000	A$300,000	
4.200	2030.12.02	S		C23264AW1	SN	'23-'24	$1,500,000	$1,500,000	
2.750	2032.02.13	A	23		MN	2025	€1,500,000	€1,500,000	
3.650	2034.06.02	S		C23264AY7	SN	2024	$1,000,000	$1,000,000	
3.540	2038.04.26	A			SN	2023	NKr600,000	NKr600,000	
5.600	2039.11.25	S		125094AC6	SN	2009	US$1,250,000	US$1,250,000	
FINANCEMENT QUÉBEC									
5.250	2034.06.01	S	R	31739ZAG0	MN	'06-'10	$1,522,350	$1,522,350	

FP Bonds — Government 2025

Cpn %	Maturity	Freq	Series	CUSIP	Type	Year	Issued Amount (000)	Outstanding Amount (000)	Ref. Note
HYDRO-QUÉBEC									
F.R.	Perpetual	S	GL		BD	1986	US$400,000	US$71,630	12
F.R.	Perpetual	S	JT		BD	2023	US$128,440	US$128,440	13
6.270	2026.01.03	S	B-127	44881HEW0	MN	1996	US$50,000	US$50,000	
8.875	2026.03.01	S	GF	448814CP6	BD	1986	US$250,000	US$250,000	
8.250	2026.04.15	S	GH	448814CS0	BD	1986	US$250,000	US$250,000	
8.250	2027.01.15	S	GQ	448814CT8	BD	1987	US$250,000	US$250,000	
2.461	2027.03.02	S	0071	44889ZET9	MN	2017	$15,000	$15,000	
Z.R.	2027.04.15		0061	44889ZEH5	MN	'09-'11	$65,450	$65,450	
9.500	2027.04.30	S	B-63	44881HCK8	MN	1992	US$20,000	US$20,000	
6.625	2028.07.13	S	B-130	44881HEZ3	MN	1998	US$50,000	US$50,000	
2.000	2028.09.01	S	0082	44889ZFE1	MN	2022	$2,400,000	$2,400,000	
6.500	2029.01.16	S	0017	44889ZCK0	MN	1999	$75,000	$75,000	
Z.R.	2029.04.29		0081	44889ZFD3	MN	2021	$36,036	$36,036	
8.625	2029.06.15	S	HE	448814DB6	BD	1989	US$250,000	US$250,000	
3.400	2029.09.01	S	0086	44889ZFJ0	MN	'23-'24	$2,400,000	$2,400,000	
8.500	2029.12.01	S	HH	448814DC4	BD	1989	US$500,000	US$500,000	
9.375	2030.04.15	S	HK	448814DF7	BD	1990	US$500,000	US$500,000	
1.322	2030.06.30	S	0078	44889ZFA9	MN	2020	$35,169	$35,169	
9.500	2030.11.15	S	HQ	448814DL4	BD	1990	US$500,000	US$500,000	
11.000	2031.02.26	S	IH	448814EG4	BD	1993	$190,000	$190,000	
2.048	2031.03.02	S	0080	44889ZFC5	MN	2021	$10,000	$10,000	
Z.R.	2031.04.18		0085	44889ZFH4	MN	2022	$38,355	$38,355	
6.000	2031.08.15	S	0038	44889ZDG8	MN	2001	$30,000	$4,325	
6.000	2031.08.15	S	JG	448814GY3	BD	1999	$825,675	$825,675	14
2.729	2032.03.02	S	0083	44889ZFF8	MN	2022	$10,000	$10,000	
3.550	2032.09.01	S	0091	44889ZFP6	MN	2025	$750,000	$1,500,000	
6.500	2035.01.16	S	0009	44889ZBF2	MN	'98-'00	$686,500	$686,500	
6.400	2035.01.16	S	0011	44889ZBH8	MN	1998	$50,000	$50,000	15
3.530	2035.01.16	S	0016	44889ZCJ3	MN	1998	$170,000	$170,000	15
6.500	2035.02.15	S	0019	44889ZCM6	MN	'99-'04	$3,794,000	$3,794,000	
Z.R.	2035.07.16		0012	44889ZBJ4	MN	1998	$150,000	$150,000	15
Z.R.	2035.07.16		0014		MN	1998	$73,500	$71,000	15
Z.R.	2039.04.15		0088	44889ZFL5	MN	'23-'24	$53,135	$53,135	
6.000	2040.02.15	S	0020	44889ZCN4	MN	'99-'06	$3,770,500	$3,770,500	
5.000	2045.02.15	S	JM	448814HZ9	BD	'06-'08	$5,000,000	$5,000,000	
6.000	2050.02.15	S	0032	44889ZDA1	MN	2000	$50,000	$50,000	
5.000	2050.02.15	S	JN	448814JA2	BD	'09-'13	$7,000,000	$7,000,000	
4.000	2055.02.15	S	JQ	4488148V8	BD	'14-'20	$7,000,000	$7,000,000	
Z.R.	2060.02.15		0033	44889ZDB9	MN	'00-'01	$200,000	$200,000	15
Z.R.	2060.02.15		0037	44889ZDF0	MN	2001	$10,000	$10,000	15
Z.R.	2060.02.15		0039	44889ZDH6	MN	2001	$121,000	$121,000	
Z.R.	2060.02.15		0040	44889ZDJ2	MN	2001	$30,000	$30,000	15,16
2.100	2060.02.15	S	JR	448814JC8	DB	'20-'22	$6,500,000	$6,500,000	
4.000	2063.02.15	S	JS	448814JD6	DB	'22-'24	$8,000,000	$8,000,000	
4.000	2065.02.15	S	JU	448814BQ5	DB	'24-'25	$2,500,000	$3,500,000	

CALLABLE BONDS
March 31, 2025

Coupon Rate %	Maturity Date	Next Call Date	Next Call Price	Call Flag
CDP FINANCIAL INC.				
5.600	2039.11.25	anytime	US$100.00	C
HYDRO-QUÉBEC				
F.R.	Perpetual	2025.09.09	US$100.00	P
F.R.	Perpetual	2025.03.31	US$100.00	P

REFERENCES
1. Green bonds.
2. Was retractable on Jan. 30, 2011, 2016 and 2021.
3. Was retractable on Feb. 27, 2016.
4. Was retractable on Mar. 10, 2008. Previously, interest rate was 6.185%.
5. Extendible to Apr. 1, 2026 with an interest rate of 7.5%.
6. Extendible to Apr. 1, 2026 with an interest rate of 6.4%.
7. Was retractable on Apr. 15, 2021.
8. Was retractable on July 22, 2006 and thereafter on interest payment dates.
9. Real return bonds. The bonds pay semiannual interest plus an adjustment based on the Canadian Consumer Price Index.
10. Terms of the notes include irregular blended payments of interest and principal.
11. Was retractable on July 22, 2016.
12. Interest rate is 6-month SOFR (Secured Overnight Financing Rate) plus 0.49076%
13. Interest rate is SOFR plus 0.49076%.
14. Outstanding amount includes $25,675,000 issued upon exchange of medium term notes with like terms.
15. Discount bonds.
16. Variable rate payable annually beginning Feb. 15, 2050.

Saskatchewan

Premier: Scott Moe (Saskatchewan Party)
Capital City: Regina
Area: 651,936 sq. kilometres

Visit this Web site:
Province of Saskatchewan: www.saskatchewan.ca

DBRS Bond Rating at January 16, 2025 ... AA low

	2024	2023
Employed	608,200	607,000
Unemployment rate (%)	6	5
Average weekly earnings (Dec.)	$1,243.07	$1,170.89
Building permits	$2,698,960,000	$2,364,160,000
Retail sales	$25,880,717,000	$25,217,690,000
Population (est. July 1)	1,239,865	1,209,107
December consumer price index (2002=100)	162.8	159.9
Sales tax (GST)	5%	5%
(PST)	6%	6%

FP Bonds — Government 2025

DIRECT DEBT

March 31, 2025

Cpn %	Maturity	Freq	Series	CUSIP	Type	Year	Issued Amount (000)	Outstanding Amount (000)	Ref. Note
PROVINCE OF SASKATCHEWAN									
8.750	2025.05.30	S		803854FP8	DB	1995	$175,000	$175,000	
0.800	2025.09.02	S		803854KM9	DB	2020	$1,200,000	$1,200,000	
2.550	2026.06.02	S		803854KB3	DB	'16-'21	$1,575,000	$1,575,000	
2.650	2027.06.02	S		803854KE7	DB	2017	$1,000,000	$1,000,000	
3.250	2027.06.08	S		803854KQ0	BD	2022	US$1,000,000	US$1,000,000	
3.050	2028.12.02	S		803854KF4	DB	'18-'19	$1,300,000	$1,300,000	
5.600	2029.03.05	S		803854GZ5	MN	1999	$60,000	$60,000	
5.750	2029.03.05	S	SB	803854GY8	DB	'98-'00	$350,000	$350,000	
6.350	2030.01.25	S		803854JN9	MN	'00-'07	$200,000	$169,995	
6.250	2030.01.25	S		803854HF8	MN	2000	$25,000	$25,000	
4.650	2030.01.28	S		803854KW7	BD	2025	US$1,000,000	US$1,000,000	
2.200	2030.06.02	S	XC	803854KJ6	DB	'19-'21	$1,400,000	$1,400,000	
2.150	2031.06.02	S		803854KP2	DB	'21-'22	$1,600,000	$1,600,000	
6.400	2031.09.05	S	XB	803854HN1	DB	'01-'03	$550,000	$550,000	
6.300	2032.02.13	S		803854JR0	MN	2002	$30,000	$29,954	
0.525	2032.03.01	A			NT	2022	SFr100,000	SFr100,000	
3.900	2033.06.02	S		803854KU1	DB	'23-'24	$1,700,000	$1,700,000	
5.800	2033.09.05	S		803854JA7	DB	'03-'04	$450,000	$450,000	
5.800	2033.09.05	S		803854JB5	DB	'03-'04	$104,500	$104,500	1
1.315	2034.05.02	A			NT	2024	SFr100,000	SFr100,000	
3.300	2034.05.08	A			NT	2024	€1,250,000	€1,250,000	
5.600	2035.09.05	S	DC	803854JH2	DB	2004	$400,000	$400,000	
5.000	2037.03.05	S	EC	803854JJ8	DB	'05-'06	$425,000	$425,000	
4.750	2040.06.01	S		803854JL3	DB	'06-'10	$1,050,000	$1,050,000	
3.400	2042.02.03	S		803854JT6	DB	'12-'13	$800,000	$800,000	
5.700	2042.09.05	S		803854HY7	MN	2002	$50,000	$50,000	
3.900	2045.06.02	S	MC	803854JU3	DB	'13-'15	$1,450,000	$1,450,000	
2.750	2046.12.02	S		803854KA5	DB	'15-'16	$2,200,000	$2,200,000	
3.300	2048.06.02	S		803854KC1	DB	'16-'18	$2,125,000	$2,125,000	
3.100	2050.06.02	S		803854KH0	DB	'18-'20	$2,500,000	$2,500,000	
2.800	2052.12.02	S		803854KN7	DB	'21-'22	$1,600,000	$1,600,000	
3.750	2054.03.05	S		803854JX7	DB	'14-'17	$725,000	$725,000	
4.200	2054.12.02	S		803854KV9	DB	'23-'24	$2,000,000	$2,000,000	
2.950	2058.06.02	S		803854KG2	MN	'18-'23	$750,000	$750,000	
2.350	2060.06.02	S		803854KL1	MN	'20-'21	$310,000	$310,000	
3.800	2062.06.02	S		803854KT4	MN	2023	$300,000	$300,000	

REFERENCES
1. Extendible to Sept. 5, 2033 with an interest rate of 5.8%.

EURO BONDS
March 31, 2025

Cpn %	Maturity	Freq	Series	Year	Issued Amount (000)	Outstanding Amount (000)
CPPIB CAPITAL INC.						
F.R.	2025.04.04	Q	47	2022	US$1,500,000	US$1,500,000
6.000	2025.06.07	A	58	2023	£1,000,000	£1,000,000
4.375	2026.03.02	A	56	2023	£750,000	£750,000
F.R.	2026.03.11	Q	40	2021	US$750,000	US$750,000
F.R.	2026.06.15	Q	37	2021	£750,000	£750,000
F.R.	2026.07.27	Q	66	2024	US$500,000	US$500,000
0.250	2027.04.06	A	19	2020	€1,000,000	€1,000,000
4.500	2027.07.22	A	63	2024	£600,000	£600,000
2.750	2027.11.02	S	4	2017	US$1,000,000	US$1,000,000
4.250	2028.07.20	S	59	2023	US$1,500,000	US$1,500,000
0.875	2029.02.06	A	12	2019	€1,000,000	€1,000,000
3.125	2029.06.11	A	65	2024	€1,000,000	€1,000,000
2.000	2029.11.01	S	15	2019	US$1,000,000	US$1,000,000
1.125	2029.12.14	A	23	2020	£750,000	£750,000
0.050	2031.02.24	A	31	2021	€1,000,000	€1,000,000
2.875	2032.01.30	A	69	2025	€1,250,000	€1,250,000
1.500	2033.03.04	A	6	2018	€1,000,000	€1,000,000
0.750	2037.02.02	A	46	2022	€1,000,000	€1,000,000
0.250	2041.01.18	A	28	2021	€1,000,000	€1,000,000
2.414	2041.02.25	S		2021	A$150,000	A$150,000
2.790	2041.03.12	S	33	2021	A$120,000	A$120,000
0.750	2049.07.15	A	13	2019	€1,000,000	€1,000,000
2.580	2051.02.23	S	30	2021	A$160,000	A$160,000
1.625	2071.10.22	A	43	2021	£900,000	£900,000
PROVINCE OF ALBERTA						
0.500	2025.04.16	A		2020	€1,100,000	€1,100,000
0.625	2025.04.18	A		2018	€1,500,000	€1,500,000
0.625	2026.01.16	A		2019	€1,250,000	€1,250,000
2.050	2026.08.17	S	PAGM06	2016	US$1,000,000	US$1,000,000
0.250	2028.04.20	A		2020	SFr260,000	SFr260,000
0.375	2029.02.07	A		2019	SFr325,000	SFr325,000
1.403	2029.02.20	A		2019	SKr2,500,000	SKr2,500,000
3.125	2034.10.16	A		2024	€1,500,000	€1,500,000
1.782	2040.12.03	A		'15-'16	€202,000	€202,000
3.225	2041.09.16	S		2021	NZ$128,000	NZ$128,000
1.150	2043.12.01	A		'16-'17	€435,000	€435,000
0.925	2045.05.08	A		2020	€70,000	€70,000
1.413	2050.03.31	A		2020	€30,000	€30,000
1.500	2050.04.07	A		2020	€90,000	€90,000
PROVINCE OF BRITISH COLUMBIA						
0.875	2025.10.08	A	BCEURO-2	2015	€500,000	€500,000
4.500	2029.06.18	A	BCGBP-02	2024	£500,000	£500,000
2.500	2030.04.18	A	BCSFR-7	2010	SFr100,000	SFr100,000
0.700	2032.07.20	A	BCEURO-5	2016	€250,000	€250,000

Cpn %	Maturity	Freq	Series	Year	Issued Amount (000)	Outstanding Amount (000)
3.000	2034.07.24	A	BCEURO-17	2024	€1,850,000	€1,850,000
1.337	2037.01.27	A	BCEURO-6	2017	€150,000	€150,000
3.210	2038.11.08	A	BCEURO-1	2011	€40,000	€40,000
3.741	2039.04.01	A	BCEURO-16	2023	€100,000	€100,000
3.400	2039.05.24	A	BCEURO-18	2024	€1,500,000	€1,500,000
3.508	2039.06.07	A	BCEURO-14	2023	€86,000	€86,000
2.060	2039.06.09	A	BCEURO-13	2022	€100,000	€100,000
1.678	2040.12.18	A	BCEURO-3	2015	€75,000	€75,000
0.590	2042.12.22	A	BCEURO-12	2021	€135,000	€135,000
1.250	2043.06.17	A	BCEURO-4	2016	€100,000	€100,000
1.227	2044.04.25	A	BCEURO-7	2019	€130,000	€130,000
3.300	2046.06.28	A	BCEURO-19	2024	€50,000	€50,000
1.000	2048.04.09	A	BCEURO-11	2020	€170,000	€170,000
0.478	2049.10.18	A	BCEURO-9	'19-'23	€709,000	€709,000
0.270	2050.03.30	A	BCEURO-10	2020	€150,000	€150,000
3.402	2053.06.05	A	BCEURO-15	2023	€80,000	€80,000

PROVINCE OF MANITOBA

Cpn %	Maturity	Freq	Series	Year	Issued Amount (000)	Outstanding Amount (000)
0.200	2026.04.20	A		2020	SFr100,000	SFr100,000
0.250	2029.03.15	A		2019	SFr250,000	SFr250,000
2.915	2029.04.10	S	C169	2019	NZ$39,500	NZ$39,500
1.523	2034.05.16	A		2024	SFr130,000	SFr130,000
1.252	2034.07.18	A		2019	SKr500,000	SKr500,000
F.R.	2034.08.23	Q		2024	€50,000	€50,000
0.600	2035.03.30	A		2020	€60,000	€60,000
0.866	2035.04.16	A		2025	SFr210,000	SFr210,000
1.390	2035.06.11	A	C142	2015	€32,000	€32,000
0.750	2037.02.02	A		2022	€70,000	€70,000
3.740	2037.02.16	A		2022	NZ$130,000	NZ$130,000
0.800	2039.03.15	A		2019	SFr150,000	SFr150,000
1.000	2039.06.25	A	C154	2016	€40,000	€40,000
0.700	2040.04.20	A		2020	SFr100,000	SFr100,000
1.770	2040.06.25	A	C143	'15-'16	€470,000	€470,000
1.740	2041.02.25	A	C147	2016	€85,000	€85,000
1.500	2041.06.25	A	C151	'16-'19	€285,000	€285,000
1.950	2041.06.25	A	H062	2016	€45,000	€45,000
0.700	2041.11.25	A		2021	€160,000	€160,000
0.800	2046.04.27	S	C149	2016	Jp¥5,000,000	Jp¥5,000,000
0.700	2046.08.30	S	C153	2016	Jp¥6,000,000	Jp¥6,000,000
0.700	2046.12.05	S	C156	2016	Jp¥5,000,000	Jp¥5,000,000
1.500	2049.06.25	A	C170	2019	€100,000	€100,000
1.250	2049.06.25	A	C176	2020	€75,000	€75,000
0.475	2049.11.02	A		2020	€100,000	€100,000

PROVINCE OF NEW BRUNSWICK

Cpn %	Maturity	Freq	Series	Year	Issued Amount (000)	Outstanding Amount (000)
0.250	2029.01.19	A	HV	'17-'18	SFr300,000	SFr300,000
0.200	2031.11.07	A	HU	2016	SFr400,000	SFr400,000
0.125	2032.12.06	A	IE	2019	SFr100,000	SFr100,000
0.250	2039.12.06	A	ID	2019	SFr125,000	SFr125,000

FP Bonds — Government 2025

Cpn %	Maturity	Freq	Series	Year	Issued Amount (000)	Outstanding Amount (000)
PROVINCE OF NEWFOUNDLAND AND LABRADOR						
0.800	2033.12.19	A	E002	2024	SFr100,000	SFr100,000
3.067	2034.12.04	A	E001	2024	€50,000	€50,000
PROVINCE OF ONTARIO						
0.625	2025.04.17	A	EMTN116	2018	€1,500,000	€1,500,000
2.250	2026.05.26	A	EMTN126	2022	£500,000	£500,000
0.250	2026.12.15	A	EMTN121	2021	£1,750,000	£1,750,000
0.375	2027.04.08	A	EMTN117	2020	€1,000,000	€1,000,000
0.250	2029.06.28	A	EMTN115	2017	SFr400,000	SFr400,000
0.010	2030.11.25	A	EMTN120	2020	€2,500,000	€2,500,000
0.250	2031.06.09	A	EMTN123	2021	€1,000,000	€1,000,000
0.050	2033.05.12	A	EMTN122	2021	SFr250,000	SFr250,000
3.100	2034.01.31	A	EMTN127	2024	€1,250,000	€1,250,000
9.400	2034.07.13	S	EMTN5	1994	$300,000	$300,000
0.699	2040.10.02	A	EMTN118	2020	€50,000	€50,000
1.820	2041.06.28	A	EMTN112	2016	€52,000	€52,000
0.700	2041.12.09	A	EMTN125	2021	€75,000	€75,000
0.760	2046.12.03	A	EMTN124	2021	€160,000	€160,000
OMERS FINANCE TRUST						
0.450	2025.05.13	A		2020	€1,000,000	€1,000,000
1.100	2026.03.26	S		2021	US$1,000,000	US$1,000,000
4.000	2028.04.20	S		2023	US$1,000,000	US$1,000,000
3.125	2029.01.25	A		2024	€750,000	€750,000
4.375	2030.03.20	S		2025	US$1,000,000	US$1,000,000
3.500	2032.04.19	S		2022	US$600,000	US$600,000
5.500	2033.11.15	S		2023	US$1,000,000	US$1,000,000
3.250	2035.01.28	A		2025	€1,000,000	€1,000,000
4.000	2052.04.19	S		2022	US$500,000	US$500,000
ONTARIO TEACHERS' FINANCE TRUST						
1.375	2025.04.15	S		2020	US$1,000,000	US$1,000,000
0.500	2025.05.06	A		2020	€1,500,000	€1,500,000
1.125	2026.05.15	A		2021	£500,000	£500,000
3.000	2027.04.13	S	7	2022	US$1,500,000	US$1,500,000
4.250	2028.04.25	S	12	2023	US$1,500,000	US$1,500,000
0.100	2028.05.19	A		2021	€1,250,000	€1,250,000
3.300	2029.10.05	A		2022	€500,000	€500,000
1.250	2030.09.27	S		2020	US$1,500,000	US$1,500,000
0.050	2030.11.25	A		2020	€750,000	€750,000
2.000	2031.04.16	S		2021	US$1,500,000	US$1,500,000
1.850	2032.05.03	A		2022	€1,250,000	€1,250,000
0.900	2041.05.20	A		2021	€1,250,000	€1,250,000
0.950	2051.11.24	A		2021	€500,000	€500,000
PROVINCE OF QUÉBEC						
0.200	2025.04.07	A	E210	2020	€1,600,000	€1,600,000
1.125	2025.10.28	A	E198	2015	€1,100,000	€1,100,000
2.250	2026.09.15	A	E215	2022	£750,000	£750,000
0.875	2027.05.04	A	E200	2017	€2,250,000	€2,250,000
1.305	2028.03.21	S	E192	2013	Jp¥5,000,000	Jp¥5,000,000
0.875	2028.07.05	A	E203	2018	€1,000,000	€1,000,000

Eurobonds

Cpn %	Maturity	Freq	Series	Year	Issued Amount (000)	Outstanding Amount (000)
2.730	2029.04.03	S	E187	2009	Jp¥13,000,000	Jp¥13,000,000
2.854	2029.04.10	S	E206	2019	NZ$66,000	NZ$66,000
1.169	2029.04.11	A	E207	2019	SKr1,700,000	SKr1,700,000
2.900	2029.04.27	S	E189	2009	Jp¥3,000,000	Jp¥3,000,000
Z.R.	2029.10.15	A	E209	2019	€1,000,000	€1,000,000
4.750	2030.01.22	A	E221	2025	£750,000	£750,000
4.140	2030.03.12	A	QH	2010	€75,000	€75,000
4.020	2030.04.29	A	QI	2010	€35,000	€35,000
Z.R.	2030.10.29	A	E211	2020	€2,250,000	€2,250,000
0.250	2031.05.05	A	E212	2021	€2,500,000	€2,500,000
0.030	2031.06.18	A	E213	2021	SFr250,000	SFr250,000
3.500	2031.12.15	A	QL	2011	€27,000	€27,000
0.500	2032.01.25	A	E214	2022	€2,250,000	€2,250,000
3.000	2033.01.24	A	E216	2023	€2,250,000	€2,250,000
2.040	2033.05.09	A	E217	2023	SFr390,000	SFr390,000
3.125	2034.03.27	A	E218	2024	€2,250,000	€2,250,000
1.367	2034.04.26	A	E219	2024	SFr290,000	SFr290,000
3.350	2039.07.23	A	E220	2024	€1,250,000	€1,250,000

CDP FINANCIAL INC.

Cpn %	Maturity	Freq	Series	Year	Issued Amount (000)	Outstanding Amount (000)
F.R.	2025.05.19	Q		2023	US$500,000	US$500,000
0.875	2025.06.10			2020	US$2,500,000	US$2,500,000
1.000	2026.05.26	S	5	2021	US$1,000,000	US$1,000,000
1.750	2027.02.01	S	7	2022	US$1,500,000	US$1,500,000
1.125	2027.04.06	A		2022	€2,000,000	€2,000,000
4.250	2028.07.25	S	16	2023	US$1,500,000	US$1,500,000
3.000	2029.04.11	A		2024	€1,500,000	€1,500,000
4.625	2030.01.24	S		2025	US$1,500,000	US$1,500,000
4.376	2030.05.15	S		2023	A$300,000	A$300,000
2.750	2032.02.13	A	23	2025	€1,500,000	€1,500,000
3.540	2038.04.26	A		2023	NKr600,000	NKr600,000

HYDRO-QUÉBEC

Cpn %	Maturity	Freq	Series	Year	Issued Amount (000)	Outstanding Amount (000)
F.R.	Perpetual	S	GL	1986	US$400,000	US$71,630
F.R.	Perpetual	S	JT	2023	US$128,440	US$128,440

PROVINCE OF SASKATCHEWAN

Cpn %	Maturity	Freq	Series	Year	Issued Amount (000)	Outstanding Amount (000)
0.525	2032.03.01	A		2022	SFr100,000	SFr100,000
1.315	2034.05.02	A		2024	SFr100,000	SFr100,000
3.300	2034.05.08	A		2024	€1,250,000	€1,250,000

CANADA'S INFORMATION RESOURCE CENTRE (CIRC)

Access all these great resources online, all the time, at Canada's Information Resource Centre (CIRC)
http://circ.greyhouse.ca

Canada's Information Resource Centre (CIRC) integrates all of Grey House Canada's award-winning reference content into one easy-to-use online resource. With **over 100,000 Canadian organizations** and **over 140,600 contacts**, plus thousands of additional facts and figures, CIRC is the most comprehensive resource for specialized database content in Canada! Access all 20 databases, including the recently revised *Careers & Employment Canada*, with Canada Info Desk Complete - it's the total package!

KEY ADVANTAGES OF CIRC:

- Seamlessly cross-database search content from select databases
- Save search results for future reference
- Link directly to websites or email addresses
- Clear display of your results makes compiling and adding to your research easier than ever before

DESIGN YOUR OWN CUSTOM CONTACT LISTS!

CIRC gives you the option to define and extract your own lists in seconds. Find new business leads, do keyword searches, locate upcoming conference attendees; all the information you want is right at your fingertips.

Brand new Major Canadian Cities data!

CHOOSE BETWEEN KEYWORD AND ADVANCED SEARCH!

With CIRC, you can choose between Keyword and Advanced search to pinpoint information. Designed for both beginner and advanced researchers, you can conduct simple text searches as well as powerful Boolean searches.

PROFILES IN CIRC INCLUDE:

- Phone numbers, email addresses, fax numbers and full addresses for all branches of the organization
- Social media accounts, such as Twitter and Facebook
- Key contacts based on job titles
- Budgets, membership fees, staff sizes and more!

Search CIRC using common or unique fields, customized to your needs!

ONLY GREY HOUSE DIRECTORIES PROVIDE SPECIAL CONTENT YOU WON'T FIND ANYWHERE ELSE!

- **Associations Canada:** finances/funding sources, activities, publications, conferences, membership, awards, member profile
- **Canadian Parliamentary Guide:** private and political careers of elected members, complete list of constituencies and representatives
- **Financial Services:** type of ownership, number of employees, year founded, assets, revenue, ticker symbol
- **Libraries Canada:** staffing, special collections, services, year founded, national library symbol, regional system
- **Governments Canada:** municipal population
- **Canadian Who's Who:** birth city, publications, education (degrees, alma mater), career/occupation and employer
- **Major Canadian Cities:** demographics, ethnicity, immigration, language, education, housing, income, labour and transportation
- **Health Guide Canada:** chronic and mental illnesses, general resources, appendices and statistics
- **Cannabis Canada:** firm type, foreign activity, type of ownership, revenue sources
- **Canadian Environmental Resource Guide:** organization scope, budget, number of employees, activities, regulations, areas of environmental specialty
- **Careers & Employment Canada:** career associations, career employment websites, expanded employers, recruiters, awards and scholarships, and summer jobs
- **FP Directory of Directors:** names, directorships, educational and professional backgrounds and email addresses of top Canadian directors; list of major companies and complete company contact information
- **FPbonds:** bond information in PDF form and with sortable tables
- **FPsurvey:** detailed profiles of current publicly traded companies, as well as past corporate changes

The new CIRC provides easier searching and faster, more pinpointed results of all of our great resources in Canada, from Associations and Government to Major Companies to Zoos and everything in between. Whether you need fully detailed information on your contact or just an email address, you can customize your search query to meet your needs.

Contact us now for a **free trial** subscription or visit http://circ.greyhouse.ca

For more information please contact Grey House Publishing Canada
Tel.: (866) 433-4739 or (416) 644-6479 Fax: (416) 644-1904 | info@greyhouse.ca | www.greyhouse.ca

CENTRE DE DOCUMENTATION DU CANADA (CDC)

Consultez en tout temps toutes ces excellentes ressources en ligne grâce au Centre de documentation du Canada (CDC) à http://circ.greyhouse.ca

Le Centre de documentation du Canada (CDC) regroupe sous une seule ressource en ligne conviviale tout le contenu des ouvrages de référence primés de Grey House Canada. Répertoriant plus de **100 000 entreprises canadiennes, et plus de 140 600 personnes-ressources**, faits et chiffres, il s'agit de la ressource la plus complète en matière de bases de données spécialisées au Canada! Grâce à l'ajout de sept bases de données, le Canada Info Desk Complete est plus avantageux que jamais alors qu'il coûte 50 % que l'abonnement aux ouvrages individuels. Accédez aux 20 bases de données dès maintenant – le Canadian Info Desk Complete vous offre un ensemble complet!

PRINCIPAUX AVANTAGES DU CDC

- Recherche transversale efficace dans le contenu des bases de données
- Sauvegarde des résultats de recherche pour consultation future
- Lien direct aux sites Web et aux adresses électroniques
- Grâce à l'affichage lisible de vos résultats, il est dorénavant plus facile de compiler les résultats ou d'ajouter des critères à vos recherches

Nouvelles données sur les Principales villes canadiennes!

CONCEPTION PERSONNALISÉE DE VOS LISTES DE PERSONNES-RESSOURCES!

Le CDC vous permet de définir et d'extraire vos propres listes, et ce, en quelques secondes. Découvrez des clients potentiels, effectuez des recherches par mot-clé, trouvez les participants à une conférence à venir : l'information dont vous avez besoin, au bout de vos doigts.

CHOISISSEZ ENTRE RECHERCHES MOT-CLÉ ET AVANCÉE!

Grâce au CDC, vous pouvez choisir entre une recherche Mot-clé ou Avancée pour localiser l'information avec précision. Vous avez la possibilité d'effectuer des recherches en texte simple ou booléennes puissantes – les recherches sont conçues à l'intention des chercheurs débutants et avancés.

LES PROFILS DU CDC COMPRENNENT :

- Numéros de téléphone, adresses électroniques, numéros de télécopieur et adresses complètes pour toutes les succursales d'un organisme
- Comptes de médias sociaux, comme Twitter et Facebook
- Personnes-ressources clés en fonction des appellations d'emploi
- Budgets, frais d'adhésion, tailles du personnel et plus!

Effectuez des recherches dans le CDC à l'aide de champs uniques ou communs, personnalisés selon vos besoins!

SEULS LES RÉPERTOIRES DE GREY HOUSE VOUS OFFRENT UN CONTENU PARTICULIER QUE VOUS NE TROUVEREZ NULLE PART AILLEURS!

- **Le répertoire des associations du Canada** : sources de financement, activités, publications, congrès, membres, prix, profil de membre
- **Guide parlementaire canadien** : carrières privées et politiques des membres élus, liste complète des comtés et des représentants
- **Services financiers** : type de propriétaire, nombre d'employés, année de la fondation, immobilisations, revenus, symbole au téléscripteur
- **Bibliothèques Canada** : personnel, collections particulières, services, année de la fondation, symbole de bibliothèque national, système régional
- **Gouvernements du Canada** : population municipale
- **Canadian Who's Who** : ville d'origine, publication, formation (diplômes et alma mater), carrière/emploi et employeur
- **Principales villes canadiennes** : données démographiques, ethnicité, immigration, langue, éducation, logement, revenu, main-d'œuvre et transport
- **Guide canadien de la santé** : maladies chroniques et mentales, ressources generales, annexes et statistiques
- **Cannabis au Canada** : type d'entreprise, activité à l'étranger, type de propriété, sources de revenus
- **Guide des ressources environnementales canadiennes** : périmètre organisationnel, budget, nombre d'employés, activités, réglementations, domaines de spécialité environnementale
- **Carrières et emplois Canada** : associations professionnelles, sites Web d'emplois, employeurs, recruteurs, bourses, et emplois d'été
- **Répertoire des administrateurs** : prénom, nom de famille, poste de cadre et d'administrateur, parcours scolaire et professionnel et adresse électronique des cadres supérieurs canadiens; liste des sociétés les plus importantes au Canada et l'information complète des compagnies
- **FPbonds** : information sur les obligations en format PDF, avec tableaux à trier
- **FPsurvey** : profils détaillés de sociétés cotées en bourse et changements organisationnels antérieurs

Le nouveau CDC facilite la recherche au sein de toutes nos ressources au Canada et procure plus rapidement des résultats plus poussés – des associations au gouvernement en passant par les principales entreprises et les zoos, sans oublier tout un éventail d'organisations! Que vous ayez besoin d'information très détaillée au sujet de votre personne-ressource ou d'une simple adresse électronique, vous pouvez personnaliser votre requête afin qu'elle réponde à vos besoins. Contactez-nous sans tarder pour obtenir un **essai gratuit** ou visitez http://circ.greyhouse.ca

Pour obtenir plus d'information, veuillez contacter **Grey House Publishing Canada** par tél. : 1 866 433-4739 ou 416 644-6479 par téléc. : 416 644-1904 | info@greyhouse.ca | www.greyhouse.ca

Canadian Almanac & Directory
The Definitive Resource for Facts & Figures About Canada

The *Canadian Almanac & Directory* has been Canada's most authoritative sourcebook for 178 years. Published annually since 1847, it continues to be widely used by publishers, business professionals, government offices, researchers, information specialists and anyone needing current, accessible information on every imaginable topic relevant to those who live and work in Canada.

A directory and a guide, the *Canadian Almanac & Directory* provides the most comprehensive picture of Canada, from physical attributes to economic and business summaries, leisure and recreation. It combines textual materials, charts, colour photographs and directory listings with detailed profiles, all verified and organized for easy retrieval. The *Canadian Almanac & Directory* is a wealth of general information, displaying national statistics on population, employment, CPI, imports and exports, as well as images of national awards, Canadian symbols, flags, emblems and Canadian parliamentary leaders.

For important contacts throughout Canada, for any number of business projects or for that once-in-a-while critical fact, the *Canadian Almanac & Directory* will help you find the leads you didn't even know existed—quickly and easily!

ALL THE INFORMATION YOU'LL EVER NEED, ORGANIZED INTO 17 DISTINCT CATEGORIES FOR EASY NAVIGATION!

Almanac—a fact-filled snapshot of Canada, including History, Geography, Economics and Vital Statistics.

Arts & Culture—includes 9 topics from Galleries to Zoos.

Associations—thousands of organizations arranged in over 120 different topics, from Accounting to Youth.

Broadcasting—Canada's major Broadcasting Companies, Provincial Radio and Television Stations, Cable Companies, and Specialty Broadcasters.

Business & Finance—Accounting, Banking, Insurance, Canada's Major Companies and Stock Exchanges.

Education—arranged by Province and includes Districts, Government Agencies, Specialized and Independent Schools, Universities and Technical facilities.

Government—spread over three sections, with a Quick Reference Guide, Federal and Provincial listings, County and Municipal Districts and coverage of Courts in Canada.

Health—Government agencies, hospitals, community health centres, retirement care and mental health facilities.

Law Firms—all Major Law Firms, followed by smaller firms organized by Province and listed alphabetically.

Libraries—Canada's main Library/Archive and Government Departments for Libraries, followed by Provincial listings and Regional Systems.

Publishing—Books, Magazines and Newspapers organized by Province, including frequency and circulation figures.

Religion—broad information about religious groups and associations from 37 different denominations.

Sports—Associations in 110 categories, with detailed League and Team listings.

Transportation—complete listings for all major modes.

Utilities—Associations, Government Agencies and Provincial Utility Companies.

PRINT OR ONLINE—QUICK AND EASY ACCESS TO ALL THE INFORMATION YOU NEED!

Available in hardcover print or electronically via the web, the *Canadian Almanac & Directory* provides instant access to the people you need and the facts you want every time.

Canadian Almanac & Directory print edition is verified and updated annually. Ongoing changes are added to the web version on a regular basis. The web version allows you to narrow your search by using index fields such as name or type of organization, subject, location, contact name or title and postal code.

Online subscribers have the option to instantly generate their own contact lists and export them into spreadsheets for further use—a great alternative to high cost list broker services.

 For more information please contact Grey House Publishing Canada
Tel.: (866)-433-4739 or (416) 644-6479 Fax: (416) 644-1904 | info@greyhouse.ca | www.greyhouse.ca

Répertoire et almanach canadien
La ressource de référence au sujet des données et des faits relatifs au Canada

Le *Répertoire et almanach canadien* constitue le guide canadien le plus rigoureux depuis 178 ans. Publié annuellement depuis 1847, il est toujours grandement utilisé dans le monde des affaires, les bureaux gouvernementaux, par les spécialistes de l'information, les chercheurs, les éditeurs ou quiconque est à la recherche d'information actuelle et accessible sur tous les sujets imaginables à propos des gens qui vivent et travaillent au Canada.

À la fois répertoire et guide, le *Répertoire et almanach canadien* dresse le tableau le plus complet du Canada, des caractéristiques physiques jusqu'aux revues économique et commerciale, en passant par les loisirs et les activités récréatives. Il combine des documents textuels, des représentations graphiques, des photographies en couleurs et des listes de répertoires accompagnées de profils détaillés. Autant d'information pointue et organisée de manière à ce qu'elle soit facile à obtenir. Le *Répertoire et almanach canadien* foisonne de renseignements généraux. Il présente des statistiques nationales sur la population, l'emploi, l'IPC, l'importation et l'exportation ainsi que des images des prix nationaux, des symboles canadiens, des drapeaux, des emblèmes et des leaders parlementaires canadiens.

Si vous cherchez des personnes-ressources essentielles un peu partout au Canada, peu importe qu'il s'agisse de projets d'affaires ou d'une question factuelle anecdotique, le *Répertoire et almanach canadien* vous fournira les pistes dont vous ignoriez l'existence – rapidement et facilement!

TOUTE L'INFORMATION DONT VOUS AUREZ BESOIN, ORGANISÉE EN 17 CATÉGORIES DISTINCTES POUR UNE CONSULTATION FACILE!

Almanach—un aperçu informatif du Canada, notamment l'histoire, la géographie, l'économie et les statistiques essentielles.

Arts et culture—comprends 9 sujets, des galeries aux zoos.

Associations—des milliers d'organisations classées selon plus de 120 sujets différents, de l'actuariat au jeunesse.

Radiodiffusion—les principales sociétés de radiodiffusion au Canada, les stations radiophoniques et de télévision ainsi que les entreprises de câblodistribution et les diffuseurs thématiques.

Commerce et finance—comptabilité, services bancaires, assurances, principales entreprises et bourses canadiennes.

Éducation—organisé par province et comprend les arrondissements scolaires, les organismes gouvernementaux, les écoles spécialisées et indépendantes, les universités et établissements techniques.

Gouvernement—s'étend sur trois sections et comprend un guide de référence, des listes fédérales et provinciales, les comtés et arrondissements municipaux ainsi que les cours canadiennes.

Santé—organismes gouvernementaux, hôpitaux, centres de santé communautaires, établissements de soins pour personnes retraitées et de soins de santé mentale.

Sociétés d'avocats—toutes les principales sociétés d'avocats, suivies des sociétés plus petites, classées par province et en ordre alphabétique.

Bibliothèques—la bibliothèque et les archives principales du Canada ainsi que les bibliothèques des ministères, suivis des listes provinciales et des systèmes régionaux.

Édition—livres, magazines et journaux classés par province, y compris leur fréquence et les données relatives à leur diffusion.

Religion—information générale au sujet des groupes religieux et des associations religieuses de 37 dénominations.

Sports—associations de 110 sports distincts; comprend des listes de ligues et d'équipes.

Transport—des listes complètes des principaux modes de transport.

Services publics—associations, organismes gouvernementaux et entreprises de services publics provinciaux.

FORMAT PAPIER OU EN LIGNE – ACCÈS RAPIDE À TOUS LES RENSEIGNEMENTS DONT VOUS AVEZ BESOIN!

Offert sous couverture rigide ou en format électronique grâce au web, le *Répertoire et almanach canadien* offre invariablement un accès instantané aux représentants du gouvernement et aux faits qui font l'objet de vos recherches.

La version imprimée du Répertoire et almanach canadien est vérifiée et mise à jour annuellement. La version en ligne est mise à jour mensuellement. Cette version vous permet de circonscrire la recherche grâce aux champs de l'index comme le nom ou le type d'organisme, le sujet, l'emplacement, le nom ou le titre de la personne-ressource et le code postal.

Les abonnés au service en ligne peuvent générer instantanément leurs propres listes de contacts et les exporter en format feuille de calcul pour une utilisation approfondie – une solution de rechange géniale aux services dispendieux d'un commissionnaire en publipostage.

 Pour obtenir plus d'information, veuillez contacter **Grey House Publishing Canada** par tél. : 1 866 433-4739 ou 416 644-6479 par téléc. : 416 644-1904 | info@greyhouse.ca | www.greyhouse.ca

Canadian Who's Who

Canadian Who's Who is the only authoritative publication of its kind in Canada, offering access to the top 10,000 notable Canadians in all walks of life. Published annually to provide current and accurate information, the familiar bright-red volume is recognized as the standard reference source of contemporary Canadian biography.

Documenting the achievement of Canadians from a wide variety of occupations and professions, *Canadian Who's Who* records the diversity of culture in Canada. These biographies are organized alphabetically and provide detailed information on the accomplishments of notable Canadians, from coast to coast. All who are interested in the achievements of Canada's most influential citizens and their significant contributions to the country and the world beyond should acquire this reference title.

Detailed entries give date and place of birth, education, family details, career information, memberships, creative works, honours, languages, and awards, together with full addresses. Included are outstanding Canadians from business, academia, politics, sports, the arts and sciences, etc.

Every year the publisher invites new individuals to complete questionnaires from which new biographies are compiled. The publisher also gives those already listed in earlier editions an opportunity to update their biographies. Those listed are selected because of the positions they hold in Canadian society, or because of the contributions they have made to Canada.

AVAILABLE ONLINE!

Canadian Who's Who is also available online, through Canada's Information Resource Centre (CIRC). Readers can access this title's in-depth and vital networking content in the format that best suits their needs—in print, by subscription or online.

The print edition of *Canadian Who's Who 2025* contains 10,000 entries, while the online edition gives users access to over 27,800 biographies, including all current listings and over 16,500 archived biographies dating back to 1999.

 For more information please contact Grey House Publishing Canada
Tel.: (866)-433-4739 or (416) 644-6479 Fax: (416) 644-1904 | info@greyhouse.ca | www.greyhouse.ca

Canadian Who's Who

Canadian Who's Who est la seule publication digne de foi de son genre au Canada. Elle donne accès 10 000 dignitaires canadiens de tous les horizons. L'ouvrage annuel rouge vif bien connu, rempli d'information à jour et exacte, est la référence standard en matière de biographies canadiennes contemporaines.

Canadian Who's Who, qui porte sur les réalisations de Canadiens occupant une vaste gamme de postes et de professions, illustre la diversité de la culture canadienne. Ces biographies sont classées en ordre alphabétique et donnent de l'information détaillée sur les réalisations de Canadiens éminents, d'un océan à l'autre. Tous ceux qui s'intéressent aux réalisations des citoyens les plus influents au Canada et à leurs contributions importantes au pays et partout dans le monde doivent se procurer cet ouvrage de référence.

Les entrées détaillées indiquent la date et le lieu de la naissance, traitent de l'éducation, de la famille, de la carrière, des adhésions, des œuvres de création, des distinctions, des langues et des prix - en plus des adresses complètes. Elles comprennent des Canadiens exceptionnels du monde des affaires, des universités, de la politique, des sports, des arts, des sciences et plus encore!

Chaque année, l'éditeur invite de nouvelles personnes à remplir les questionnaires à partir desquels il prépare les nouvelles biographies. Il le remet également aux personnes qui font partie de numéros antérieurs afin de leur permettre d'effectuer une mise à jour. Les personnes retenues le sont en raison des postes qu'elles occupent dans la société canadienne ou de leurs contributions au Canada.

OFFERT EN FORMAT ÉLECTRONIQUE!

Canadian Who's Who est également offert en ligne par l'entremise du Centre de documentation du Canada (CDC). Les lecteurs peuvent accéder au contenu approfondi et essentiel au réseautage de cet ouvrage dans le format qui leur convient le mieux - version imprimée, en ligne ou par abonnement.

L'édition imprimée de *Canadian Who's Who 2025* compte 10 000 entrées tandis qu'en consultant la version en ligne, les utilisateurs ont accès à 27 800 biographies, dont fiches d'actualité et plus de 16 500 biographies archives qui remontent jusqu'à 1999.

Pour obtenir plus d'information, veuillez contacter Grey House Publishing Canada
par tél. : 1 866 433-4739 ou 416 644-6479 par téléc. : 416 644-1904 | info@greyhouse.ca | www.greyhouse.ca

Associations Canada
Makes Researching Organizations Quick and Easy

Associations Canada is an easy-to-use compendium, providing detailed indexes, listings and abstracts on over 20,500 local, regional, provincial, national and international organizations (identifying location, budget, founding date, management, scope of activity and funding source—just to name a few).

POWERFUL INDEXES HELP YOU TARGET THE ORGANIZATIONS YOU WANT

There are a number of criteria you can use to target specific organizations. Organized with the user in mind, *Associations Canada* is broken down into a number of indexes to help you find what you're looking for quickly and easily.

- **Subject Index**—listing of Canadian and foreign association headquarters, alphabetically by subject and keyword
- **Acronym Index**—an alphabetical listing of acronyms and corresponding Canadian and foreign associations, in both official languages
- **Budget Index**—Canadian associations, alphabetical within eight budget categories
- **Conferences & Conventions Index**—meetings sponsored by Canadian and foreign associations, listed alphabetically by conference name
- **Executive Name Index**—alphabetical listing of key contacts of Canadian associations, for both headquarters and branches
- **Geographic Index**—listing of headquarters, branch offices, chapters and divisions of Canadian associations, alphabetical within province and city
- **Mailing List Index**—associations that offer mailing lists, alphabetical by subject
- **Registered Charitable Organizations Index**—listing of associations that are registered charities, alphabetical by subject

PRINT OR ONLINE – QUICK AND EASY ACCESS TO ALL THE INFORMATION YOU NEED!

Available in softcover print or electronically via the web, *Associations Canada* provides instant access to the people you need and the facts you want every time. Whereas the print edition is verified and updated annually, ongoing changes are added to the web version on a regular basis. The web version allows you to narrow your search by using index fields such as name or type of organization, subject, location, contact name or title and postal code.

Create your own contact lists! Online subscribers have the option to instantly generate their own contact lists and export them into spreadsheets for further use—a great alternative to high cost list broker services.

ASSOCIATIONS CANADA PROVIDES COMPLETE ACCESS TO THESE HIGHLY LUCRATIVE MARKETS:

Travel & Tourism
- Who's hosting what event...when and where?
- Check on events up to three years in advance

Journalism and Media
- Pure research—What do they do? Who is in charge? What's their budget?
- Check facts and sources in one step

Libraries
- Refer researchers to the most complete Canadian association reference anywhere

Business
- Target your market, research your interests, compile profiles and identify membership lists
- Warm up your cold calls with all the background you need to sell your product or service
- Preview prospects by budget, market interest or geographic location

Association Executives
- Look for strategic alliances with associations of similar interest
- Spot opportunities or conflicts with convention plans

Research & Government
- Scan interest groups or identify charities in your area of concern
- Check websites, publications and speaker availability
- Evaluate mandates, affiliations and scope

 For more information please contact Grey House Publishing Canada
Tel.: (866)-433-4739 or (416) 644-6479 Fax: (416) 644-1904 | info@greyhouse.ca | www.greyhouse.ca

Associations du Canada
La recherche d'organisations simplifiée

Il s'agit d'un recueil facile d'utilisation qui offre des index, des fiches descriptives et des résumés exhaustifs de plus de 20 500 organismes locaux, régionaux, provinciaux, nationaux et internationaux. Il donne, entre autres, des détails sur leur emplacement, leur budget, leur date de mise sur pied, l'éventail de leurs activités et leurs sources de financement.

En plus d'affecter plus d'un milliard de dollars annuellement aux frais de transport, à la participation à des congrès et à la mise en marché, *Associations du Canada* débourse des millions de dollars dans sa quête pour répondre aux intérêts de ses membres.

DES INDEX PUISSANTS QUI VOUS AIDENT À CIBLER LES ORGANISATIONS VOULUES

Vous pouvez vous servir de plusieurs critères pour cibler des organisations précises. C'est avec l'utilisateur en tête qu'*Associations du Canada* a été divisé en plusieurs index pour vous aider à trouver, rapidement et facilement, ce que vous cherchez.

- **Index des sujets**—liste des sièges sociaux d'associations canadiennes et étrangères; sujets classés en ordre alphabétique et mot-clé.
- **Index des acronymes**—liste alphabétique des acronymes et des associations canadiennes et étrangères équivalentes; présenté dans les deux langues officielles.
- **Index des budgets**—associations canadiennes classées en ordre alphabétique parmi huit catégories de budget.
- **Index des congrès**—rencontres commanditées par des associations canadiennes et étrangères; classées en ordre alphabétique selon le titre de l'événement.
- **Index des directeurs**—liste alphabétique des principales personnes-ressources des associations canadiennes, aux sièges sociaux et aux succursales.
- **Index géographique**—liste des sièges sociaux, des succursales, des sections régionales et des divisions des associations canadiennes; ordre alphabétique au sein des provinces et des villes.
- **Index des listes de distribution**—liste des associations qui offrent des listes de distribution; en ordre alphabétique selon le sujet.
- **Index des œuvres de bienfaisance enregistrées**—liste des associations enregistrées en tant qu'œuvres de bienfaisance; en ordre alphabétique selon le sujet.

OFFERT EN FORMAT PAPIER OU EN LIGNE – UN ACCÈS RAPIDE ET FACILE À TOUS LES RENSEIGNEMENTS DONT VOUS AVEZ BESOIN!

Offert sous couverture souple ou en format électronique grâce au web, *Associations du Canada* donne invariablement un accès instantané aux personnes et aux faits dont vous avez besoin. Si la version imprimée est vérifiée et mise à jour annuellement, des changements continus sont apportés mensuellement à la base de données en ligne. Servez-vous de la version en ligne afin de circonscrire vos recherches grâce à des champs spéciaux de l'index comme le nom de l'organisation ou son type, le sujet, l'emplacement, le nom de la personne-ressource ou son titre et le code postal.

Créez vos propres listes! Les abonnés au service en ligne peuvent générer instantanément leurs propres listes de contacts et les exporter en format feuille de calcul pour une utilisation approfondie – une solution de rechange géniale aux services dispendieux d'un commissionnaire en publipostage.

ASSOCIATIONS DU CANADA OFFRE UN ACCÈS COMPLET À CES MARCHÉS HAUTEMENT LUCRATIFS

Voyage et tourisme
- Renseignez-vous sur les hôtes des événements, sur les dates et les endroits.
- Consultez les événements trois ans au préalable.

Journalisme et médias
- Recherche authentique—quel est leur centre d'activité? Qui est la personne responsable? Quel est leur budget?
- Vérifiez les faits et sources en une seule étape.

Bibliothèques
- Orientez les chercheurs vers la référence la plus complète en ce qui concerne les associations canadiennes.

Commerce
- Ciblez votre marché, faites une recherche selon vos sujets de prédilection, compilez des profils et recensez des listes de membres.
- Préparez votre sollicitation au hasard en obtenant les renseignements dont vous avez besoin pour offrir votre produit ou service.
- Obtenez un aperçu de vos clients potentiels selon les budgets, les intérêts au marché ou l'emplacement géographique.

Directeurs d'associations
- Recherchez des alliances stratégiques avec des associations partageant vos intérêts.
- Repérez des occasions ou des conflits dans le cadre de la planification des congrès.

Recherche et gouvernement
- Parcourez les groupes d'intérêts ou identifiez les organismes de bienfaisance de votre domaine d'intérêt.
- Consultez les sites Web, les publications et vérifiez la disponibilité des conférenciers.
- Évaluez les mandats, les affiliations et le champ d'application.

 Pour obtenir plus d'information, veuillez contacter **Grey House Publishing Canada** par tél. : 1 866 433-4739 ou 416 644-6479 par téléc. : 416 644-1904 | info@greyhouse.ca | www.greyhouse.ca

Canadian Parliamentary Guide
Your Number One Source for All General Federal Elections Results!

Published annually since before Confederation, the *Canadian Parliamentary Guide* is an indispensable directory, providing biographical information on elected and appointed members in federal and provincial government. Featuring government institutions such as the Governor General's Household, Privy Council and Canadian legislature, this comprehensive collection provides historical and current election results with statistical, provincial and political data.

AVAILABLE IN PRINT AND NOW ONLINE!

THE CANADIAN PARLIAMENTARY GUIDE IS BROKEN DOWN INTO FIVE COMPREHENSIVE CATEGORIES

Monarchy—biographical information on His Majesty King Charles III, The Royal Family and the Governor General

Federal Government—a separate chapter for each of the Privy Council, Senate and House of Commons (including a brief description of the institution, its history in both text and chart format and a list of current members), followed by unparalleled biographical sketches*

General Elections

1867–2021

- information is listed alphabetically by province then by riding name
- notes on each riding include: date of establishment, date of abolition, former division and later divisions, followed by election year and successful candidate's name and party
- by-election information follows

2025

- information for the 2025 election is organized in the same manner but also includes information on all the candidates who ran in each riding, their party affiliation and the number of votes won

Provincial and Territorial Governments—Each provincial chapter includes:
- statistical information
- description of Legislative Assembly
- biographical sketch of the Lieutenant Governor or Commissioner
- list of current Cabinet Members
- dates of legislatures since confederation
- current Members and Constituencies
- biographical sketches*
- general election and by-election results, including the most recent provincial and territorial elections.

Courts: Federal—each court chapter includes a description of the court (Supreme, Federal, Federal Court of Appeal, Court Martial Appeal and Tax Court), its history and a list of its judges followed by biographical sketches*

* Biographical sketches follow a concise yet in-depth format:

Personal Data—place of birth, education, family information

Political Career—political career path and services

Private Career—work history, organization memberships, military history

Available in hardcover print, the *Canadian Parliamentary Guide* is also available electronically via the Web, providing instant access to the government officials you need and the facts you want every time. Use the web version to narrow your search with index fields such as institution, province and name.

Create your own contact lists! Online subscribers can instantly generate their own contact lists and export information into spreadsheets for further use. A great alternative to high cost list broker services!

 For more information please contact Grey House Publishing Canada
Tel.: (866)-433-4739 or (416) 644-6479 Fax: (416) 644-1904 | info@greyhouse.ca | www.greyhouse.ca

Guide parlementaire canadien

Votre principale source d'information en matière de résultats d'élections fédérales!

Publié annuellement depuis avant la Confédération, le *Guide parlementaire canadien* est une source fondamentale de notices biographiques des membres élus et nommés aux gouvernements fédéral et provinciaux. Il y est question, notamment, d'établissements gouvernementaux comme la résidence du gouverneur général, le Conseil privé et la législature canadienne. Ce recueil exhaustif présente les résultats historiques et actuels accompagnés de données statistiques, provinciales et politiques.

OFFERT EN FORMAT PAPIER ET DÉSORMAIS ÉLECTRONIQUE!

LE GUIDE PARLEMENTAIRE CANADIEN EST DIVISÉ EN CINQ CATÉGORIES EXHAUSTIVES:

La monarchie—des renseignements biographiques sur Sa Majesté le Roi Charles III, la famille royale et le gouverneur général.

Le gouvernement fédéral—un chapitre distinct pour chacun des sujets suivants: Conseil privé, sénat, Chambre des communes (y compris une brève description de l'institution, son historique sous forme de textes et de graphiques et une liste des membres actuels) suivi de notes biographiques sans pareil.*

Les élections fédérales

1867–2021

- Les renseignements sont présentés en ordre alphabétique par province puis par circonscription.
- Les notes de chaque circonscription comprennent : La date d'établissement, la date d'abolition, l'ancienne circonscription, les circonscriptions ultérieures, etc. puis l'année d'élection ainsi que le nom et le parti des candidats élus.
- Viennent ensuite des renseignements sur l'élection partielle.

2025

- Les renseignements de l'élection 2025 sont organisés de la même manière, mais comprennent également de l'information sur tous les candidats qui se sont présentés dans chaque circonscription, leur appartenance politique et le nombre de voix récoltées.

Gouvernements provinciaux et territoriaux—Chaque chapitre portant sur le gouvernement provincial comprend :

- des renseignements statistiques
- une description de l'Assemblée législative
- des notes biographiques sur le lieutenant-gouverneur ou le commissaire
- une liste des ministres actuels
- les dates de périodes législatives depuis la Confédération
- une liste des membres et des circonscriptions
- des notes biographiques*
- les résultats d'élections générales et partielles, y compris les dernières élections provinciales et territoriales.

Cours : fédérale—chaque chapitre comprend : une description de la cour (suprême, fédérale, cour d'appel fédérale, cour d'appel de la cour martiale et cour de l'impôt), son histoire, une liste des juges qui y siègent ainsi que des notes biographiques.*

* Les notes biographiques respectent un format concis, bien qu'approfondi :

Renseignements personnels—lieu de naissance, formation, renseignements familiaux

Carrière politique—cheminement politique et service public

Carrière privée—antécédents professionnels, membre d'organisations, antécédents militaires

Offert sous couverture rigide ou en format électronique grâce au web, le *Guide parlementaire canadien* donne invariablement un accès instantané aux représentants du gouvernement et aux faits qui font l'objet de vos recherches. Servez-vous de la version en ligne afin de circonscrire vos recherches grâce aux champs spéciaux de l'index comme l'institution, la province et le nom.

Créez vos propres listes! Les abonnés au service en ligne peuvent générer instantanément leurs propres listes de contacts et les exporter en format feuille de calcul pour une utilisation approfondie – une solution de rechange géniale aux services dispendieux d'un commissionnaire en publipostage!

 Pour obtenir plus d'information, veuillez contacter Grey House Publishing Canada
par tél. : 1 866 433-4739 ou 416 644-6479 par téléc. : 416 644-1904 | info@greyhouse.ca | www.greyhouse.ca

Directory of Directors
Your Best Source for Hard-to-Find Business Information

Since 1931, the *Financial Post Directory of Directors* has been recognizing leading Canadian companies and their execs. Today, this title is one of the most comprehensive resources for hard-to-find Canadian business information, allowing readers to access roughly 16,600 executive contacts from Canada's top 1,400 corporations. This prestigious title offers a definitive list of directorships and offices held by noteworthy Canadian business people. It also provides details on leading Canadian companies—publicly traded and privately-owned, including company name, contact information and the names of their executive officers and directors.

ACCESS THE COMPANIES & DIRECTORS YOU NEED IN NO TIME!

The updated 2025 edition of the *Directory of Directors* is jam-packed with information, including:

- **ALL-NEW front matter**: An infographic drawn from data in the book, a report on diversity disclosure practices, a report on human sustainability, and rankings from the FP500.
- **Personal listings**: First name, last name, gender, birth date, degrees, schools attended, executive positions and directorships, previous positions held, main business address and more.
- **Company listings**: Boards of directors and executive officers, head office address, phone and fax numbers, toll-free number, web and email addresses.

Powerful indexes enabling researchers to target just the information they need include:

- An **industrial classification index**: List of key Canadian companies, sorted by industry type according to the Global Industry Classification Standard (GICS®).
- A **geographic location index** grouping all companies in the Company Listings section according to the city and province/state of the head office; and
- An **alphabetical list of abbreviations** providing definitions of common abbreviations used for terms, titles, organizations, honours/fellowships and degrees throughout the Directory.

AVAILABLE ONLINE!

The Directory is also available online, through Canada's Information Resource Centre. Readers can access this title's in-depth and vital networking content in the format that best suits their needs—in print, by subscription or online.

Create your own contact lists! Online subscribers can instantly generate their own contact lists and export information into spreadsheets for further use. A great alternative to high cost list broker services!

 For more information please contact Grey House Publishing Canada
Tel.: (866)-433-4739 or (416) 644-6479 Fax: (416) 644-1904 | info@greyhouse.ca | www.greyhouse.ca

Répertoire des administrateurs

Votre source par excellence de renseignements professionnels difficiles à trouver

Depuis 1931, le Financial Post Directory of Directors (Répertoire des administrateurs du Financial Post) reconnaît les sociétés canadiennes importantes et leur haute direction. De nos jours, cet ouvrage compte parmi certaines des ressources les plus exhaustives lorsqu'il est question des renseignements d'affaires canadiens difficiles à trouver. Il permet aux lecteurs d'accéder à environ 16 600 coordonnées d'administrateurs provenant des 1 400 sociétés les plus importantes au Canada. Ce document prestigieux comprend une liste définitive des postes d'administrateurs et des fonctions que ces gens d'affaires canadiens remarquables occupent. Il offre également des détails sur des sociétés canadiennes importantes – privées ou négociées sur le marché – y compris le nom de l'entreprise, ses coordonnées et le nombre des membres de sa haute direction et de ses administrateurs.

UN ACCÈS RAPIDE ET FACILE À TOUS LES ENTREPRISES ET DIRECTEURS DONT VOUS AVEZ BESOIN!

La version mise à jour de 2025 du Répertoire des administrateurs du Financial Post est remplie d'information, notamment:

- **NOUVELLE** section de textes préliminaires –une infographie inspirée des données de l'ouvrage; un rapport sur les pratiques de divulgation de la diversité; un rapport sur la durabilité humaine; le classement le plus récent au FP500.
- **Données personnelles** – prénom, nom de famille, sexe, date de naissance, diplômes, écoles fréquentées, poste de cadre et d'administrateur, postes occupés préalablement, adresse professionnelle principale et plus encore.
- **Listes de sociétés** – conseils d'administration et cadres supérieurs, adresse du siège social, numéros de téléphone et de télécopieur, numéro sans frais, adresse électronique et site Web.

Des index puissants permettent aux utilisateurs de cibler l'information dont ils ont besoin, notamment:

- **Index de classement industriel** - énumère les sociétés classées par type d'industrie général selon le Global Industry Classification Standard (GICS^{MD}).
- l'**Index des emplacements géographiques** qui comprend toutes les sociétés de la section Liste des sociétés en fonction de la ville et de la province/de l'état où se trouve le siège social;
- une **liste des abréviations en ordre alphabétique** définit les abréviations courantes pour la terminologie, les titres, les organisations, les distinctions/fellowships et les diplômes mentionnés dans le Répertoire.

OFFERT EN FORMAT ÉLECTRONIQUE!

Le Répertoire est également accessible en ligne par l'entremise du Centre de documentation du Canada. Les lecteurs peuvent accéder au contenu approfondi et essentiel au réseautage de cet ouvrage dans le format qui leur convient le mieux - version imprimée, en ligne ou par abonnement.

Créez vos propres listes! Les abonnés au service en ligne peuvent générer instantanément leurs propres listes de contacts et les exporter en format feuille de calcul pour une utilisation approfondie – une solution de rechange géniale aux services dispendieux d'un commissionnaire en publipostage.

 Pour obtenir plus d'information, veuillez contacter Grey House Publishing Canada
par tél. : 1 866 433-4739 ou 416 644-6479 par téléc. : 416 644-1904 | info@greyhouse.ca | www.greyhouse.ca

Canadian Environmental Resource Guide
The Only Complete Guide to the Business of Environmental Management

The *Canadian Environmental Resource Guide* provides data on every aspect of the environment industry in unprecedented detail. It's one-stop searching for details on government offices and programs, information sources, product and service firms and trade fairs that pertain to the business of environmental management. All information is fully indexed and cross-referenced for easy use. The directory features current information and key contacts in Canada's environmental industry including:

ENVIRONMENTAL UP-DATE

- Information on prominent environmentalists, environmental abbreviations and a summary of recent environmental events
- Updated articles, rankings, statistics and charts on all aspects of the environmental industry
- Trade shows, conferences and seminars for the current year and beyond

ENVIRONMENTAL INDUSTRY RESOURCES

- Comprehensive listings for companies and firms producing and selling products and services in the environmental sector, including markets served, working language and percentage of revenue sources: public and private
- Environmental law firms, with lawyers' areas of speciality
- Detailed indexes by subject, geography and ISO

ENVIRONMENTAL GOVERNMENT LISTINGS

- Information on important intergovernmental offices and councils, and listings of environmental trade representatives abroad
- In-depth listings of environmental information at the municipal level, including population and number of households, water and waste treatment, landfill statistics and special by-laws and bans, as well as key environmental contacts for each municipality

Available in softcover print or electronically via the web, the *Canadian Environmental Resource Guide* provides instant access to the people you need and the facts you want every time. The *Canadian Environmental Resource Guide* is verified and updated annually. Ongoing changes are added to the web version on a regular basis.

CANADIAN ENVIRONMENTAL RESOURCE GUIDE OFFERS EVEN MORE CONTENT ONLINE!

Environmental Information Resources—Extensive listings of special libraries and thousands of environmental associations, with information on membership, environmental activities, key contacts and more.

Government Listings—Every federal and provincial department and agency influencing environmental initiatives and purchasing policies.

The web version allows you to narrow your search by using index fields such as name or type of organization, subject, location, contact name or title and postal code.

Create your own contact lists! Online subscribers have the option to instantly generate their own contact lists and export them into spreadsheets for further use—a great alternative to high cost list broker services.

 For more information please contact Grey House Publishing Canada
Tel.: (866)-433-4739 or (416) 644-6479 Fax: (416) 644-1904 | info@greyhouse.ca | www.greyhouse.ca

Guide des ressources environnementales canadiennes
Le seul guide complet dédié à la gestion de l'environnement

Le *Guide des ressources environnementales canadiennes* offre de l'information relative à tous les aspects de l'industrie de l'environnement dans les moindres détails. Il permet d'effectuer une recherche de données complètes sur les bureaux et programmes gouvernementaux, les sources de renseignements, les entreprises de produits et de services et les foires commerciales qui portent sur les activités de la gestion de l'environnement. Toute l'information est entièrement indexée et effectue un double renvoi pour une consultation facile. Le répertoire présente des renseignements actualisés et les personnes-ressources clés de l'industrie de l'environnement au Canada, y compris les suivants.

MISE À JOUR SUR L'INDUSTRIE DE L'ENVIRONNEMENT
- De l'information sur d'éminents environnementalistes, les abréviations utilisées dans le domaine de l'environnement et un résumé des événements environnementaux récents
- Des articles, des classements, des statistiques et des graphiques mis à jour sur tous les aspects de l'industrie verte
- Les salons professionnels, conférences et séminaires qui ont lieu cette année et ceux qui sont prévus

RESSOURCES DE L'INDUSTRIE ENVIRONNEMENTALE
- Des listes exhaustives des entreprises et des cabinets qui fabriquent ou offrent des produits et des services dans le domaine de l'environnement, y compris les marchés desservis, la langue de travail et la ventilation des sources de revenus – publics et privés
- Une liste complète des cabinets spécialisés en droit environnemental
- Des index selon le sujet, la géographie et la certification ISO

LISTES GOUVERNEMENTALES RELATIVES À L'ENVIRONNEMENT
- De l'information sur les bureaux et conseils intergouvernementaux importants ainsi que des listes des représentants de l'éco-commerce à l'extérieur du pays
- Des listes approfondies portant sur de l'information environnementale au palier municipal, notamment la population et le nombre de ménages, le traitement de l'eau et des déchets, des statistiques sur les décharges, des règlements et des interdictions spéciaux ainsi que des personnes-ressources clés en environnement pour chaque municipalité

Offert sous couverture rigide ou en format électronique grâce au Web, le *Guide des ressources environnementales canadiennes* offre invariablement un accès instantané aux représentants du gouvernement et aux faits qui font l'objet de vos recherches. Il est vérifié et mis à jour annuellement. La version en ligne est mise à jour mensuellement.

LE GUIDE DES RESSOURCES ENVIRONNEMENTALES CANADIENNES DONNE ACCÈS À PLUS DE CONTENU EN LIGNE!

Des ressources informationnelles sur l'environnement—Des bibliothèques et des centres de ressources spécialisés, et des milliers d'associations environnementales, avec de l'information sur l'adhésion, les activités environnementales, les personnes-ressources principales et plus encore.

Listes gouvernementales—Toutes les agences et tous les services gouvernementaux fédéraux et provinciaux qui exercent une influence sur les initiatives en matière d'environnement et de politiques d'achat.

Servez-vous de la version en ligne afin de circonscrire vos recherches grâce à des champs spéciaux de l'index comme le nom de l'organisation ou son type, le sujet, l'emplacement, le nom de la personne-ressource ou son titre et le code postal.

Créez vos propres listes! Les abonnés au service en ligne peuvent générer instantanément leurs propres listes de contacts et les exporter en format feuille de calcul pour une utilisation approfondie—une solution de rechange géniale aux services dispendieux d'un commissionnaire en publipostage.

 Pour obtenir plus d'information, veuillez contacter Grey House Publishing Canada par tél. : 1 866 433-4739 ou 416 644-6479 par téléc. : 416 644-1904 | info@greyhouse.ca | www.greyhouse.ca

Libraries Canada

Gain Access to Complete and Detailed Information on Canadian Libraries

Libraries Canada brings together the most current information from across the entire Canadian library sector, including libraries and branch libraries, educational libraries, regional systems, resource centres, archives, related periodicals, library schools and programs, provincial and governmental agencies and associations.

As the nation's leading library directory for over 35 years, *Libraries Canada* gives you access to almost 10,000 names and addresses of contacts in these institutions. Also included are valuable details such as library symbol, number of staff, operating systems, library type and acquisitions budget, hours of operation—all thoroughly indexed and easy to find.

INSTANT ACCESS TO CANADIAN LIBRARY SECTOR INFORMATION

Developed for publishers, advocacy groups, computer hardware suppliers, internet service providers and other diverse groups which provide products and services to the library community; associations that need to maintain a current list of library resources in Canada; and research departments, students and government agencies which require information about the types of services and programs available at various research institutions, *Libraries Canada* will help you find the information you need—quickly and easily.

EXPERT SEARCH OPTIONS AVAILABLE WITH ONLINE VERSION...

Available in print and online, *Libraries Canada* delivers easily accessible, quality information that has been verified and organized for easy retrieval. Five easy-to-use indexes assist you in navigating the print edition while the online version utilizes multiple index fields that help you get results.

Available on Grey House Publishing Canada's CIRC interface, you can choose between Keyword and Advanced search to pinpoint information. Designed for both novice and advanced researchers, you can conduct simple text searches as well as powerful Boolean searches, plus you can narrow your search by using index fields such as name or type of institution, headquarters, location, area code, contact name or title and postal code. Save your searches to build on at a later date or use the mark record function to view, print, e-mail or export your selected records.

Online subscribers have the option to instantly generate their own contact lists and export them into spreadsheets for further use. A great alternative to high cost list broker services.

LIBRARIES CANADA GIVES YOU ALL THE ESSENTIALS FOR EACH INSTITUTION:

Name, address, contact information, key personnel, number of staff

Collection information, type of library, acquisitions budget, subject area, special collection

User services, number of branches, hours of operation, ILL information, photocopy and microform facilities, for-fee research, Internet access

Systems information, details on electronic access, operating and online systems, Internet and e-mail software, Internet connectivity, access to electronic resources

Additional information including associations, publications and regional systems

With almost 60% of the data changing annually it has never been more important to have the latest version of *Libraries Canada*.

 For more information please contact Grey House Publishing Canada
Tel.: (866)-433-4739 or (416) 644-6479 Fax: (416) 644-1904 | info@greyhouse.ca | www.greyhouse.ca

Bibliothèques Canada

Accédez aux renseignements complets et détaillés au sujet des bibliothèques canadiennes

Bibliothèques Canada combine les renseignements les plus à jour provenant du secteur des bibliothèques de partout au Canada, y compris les bibliothèques et leurs succursales, les bibliothèques éducatives, les systèmes régionaux, les centres de ressources, les archives, les périodiques pertinents, les écoles de bibliothéconomie et leurs programmes, les organismes provinciaux et gouvernementaux ainsi que les associations.

Principal répertoire des bibliothèques depuis plus de 35 ans, *Bibliothèques Canada* vous donne accès à près de 10 000 noms et adresses de personnes-ressources pour ces établissements. Il comprend également des détails précieux comme le symbole d'identification de bibliothèque, le nombre de membres du personnel, les systèmes d'exploitation, le type de bibliothèque et le budget attribué aux acquisitions, les heures d'ouverture – autant d'information minutieusement indexée et facile à trouver.

Offert en version imprimée et en ligne, *Bibliothèques Canada* offre des renseignements de qualité, facile d'accès, qui ont été vérifiés et organisés afin de les obtenir facilement. Cinq index conviviaux vous aident dans la navigation du numéro imprimé tandis que la version en ligne vous permet de saisir plusieurs champs d'index pour vous aider à découvrir l'information voulue.

ACCÈS INSTANTANÉ AUX RENSEIGNEMENTS DU DOMAINE DES BIBLIOTHÈQUES CANADIENNES

Conçu pour les éditeurs, les groupes de revendication, les fournisseurs de matériel informatique, les fournisseurs de services Internet et autres groupes qui offrent produits et services aux bibliothèques; les associations qui ont besoin de conserver une liste à jour des ressources bibliothécaires au Canada; les services de recherche, les organismes étudiants et gouvernementaux qui ont besoin d'information au sujet des types de services et de programmes offerts par divers établissements de recherche, *Bibliothèques Canada* vous aide à trouver l'information nécessaire – rapidement et simplement.

LA VERSION EN LIGNE COMPREND DES OPTIONS DE RECHERCHE POUSSÉES...

À partir de l'interface du Centre de documentation du Canada de Grey House Publishing Canada, vous pouvez choisir entre la recherche poussée et rapide pour cibler votre information. Vous pouvez effectuer des recherches par texte simple, conçues à la fois pour les chercheurs débutants et chevronnés, ainsi que des recherches booléennes puissantes. Vous pouvez également restreindre votre recherche à l'aide des champs d'index, comme le nom ou le type d'établissement, le siège social, l'emplacement, l'indicatif régional, le nom de la personne-ressource ou son titre et le code postal. Enregistrez vos recherches pour vous en servir plus tard ou utilisez la fonction de marquage pour afficher, imprimer, envoyer par courriel ou exporter les dossiers sélectionnés.

Les abonnés au service en ligne peuvent générer instantanément leurs propres listes de contacts et les exporter en format feuille de calcul pour une utilisation approfondie – une solution de rechange géniale aux services dispendieux d'un commissionnaire en publipostage.

BIBLIOTHÈQUES CANADA VOUS DONNE TOUS LES RENSEIGNEMENTS ESSENTIELS RELATIFS À CHAQUE ÉTABLISSEMENT :

Leurs nom et adresse, les coordonnées de la personne-ressource, les membres clés du personnel, le nombre de membres du personnel

L'information relative aux collections, le type de bibliothèque, le budget attribué aux acquisitions, le domaine, les collections particulières

Les services aux utilisateurs, le nombre de succursales, les heures d'ouverture, les renseignements relatifs au PEB, les services de photocopie et de microforme, la recherche rémunérée, l'accès à Internet

L'information relative aux systèmes, des détails sur l'accès électronique, les systèmes d'exploitation et ceux en ligne, Internet et le logiciel de messagerie électronique, la connectivité à Internet, l'accès aux ressources électroniques

L'information supplémentaire, y compris les associations, les publications et les systèmes régionaux

Alors que près de 60 % des données sont modifiées annuellement, il est plus important que jamais de posséder la plus récente version de *Bibliothèques Canada*.

 Pour obtenir plus d'information, veuillez contacter Grey House Publishing Canada
par tél. : 1 866 433-4739 ou 416 644-6479 par téléc. : 416 644-1904 | info@greyhouse.ca | www.greyhouse.ca

Financial Services Canada
Unparalleled Coverage of the Canadian Financial Service Industry

With corporate listings for over 30,000 organizations and hard-to-find business information, *Financial Services Canada* is the most up-to-date source for names and contact numbers of industry professionals, senior executives, portfolio managers, financial advisors, agency bureaucrats and elected representatives.

Financial Services Canada is the definitive resource for detailed listings—providing valuable contact information including: name, title, organization, profile, associated companies, telephone and fax numbers, e-mail and website addresses. Use our online database and refine your search by stock symbol, revenue, year founded, assets, ownership type or number of employees.

POWERFUL INDEXES HELP YOU LOCATE THE CRUCIAL FINANCIAL INFORMATION YOU NEED.

Organized with the user in mind, *Financial Services Canada* contains categorized listings and 4 easy-to-use indexes:

- **Alphabetic**—financial organizations listed in alphabetical sequence by company name
- **Geographic**—financial institutions broken down by town or city
- **Executive Name**—all officers, directors and senior personnel in alphabetical order by surname
- **Insurance class**—lists all companies by insurance type

Reduce the time you spend compiling lists, researching company information and searching for e-mail addresses. Whether you are interested in contacting a finance lawyer regarding international and domestic joint ventures, need to generate a list of foreign banks in Canada or want to contact the Toronto Stock Exchange—*Financial Services Canada* gives you the power to find all the data you need.

PRINT OR ONLINE—QUICK AND EASY ACCESS TO ALL THE INFORMATION YOU NEED!

Available in softcover print or electronically via the web, *Financial Services Canada* provides instant access to the people you need and the facts you want every time.

Financial Services Canada print edition is verified and updated annually. Ongoing changes are added to the web version on a regular basis. The web version allows you to narrow your search by using index fields such as name or type of organization, subject, location, contact name or title and postal code.

Create your own contact lists! Online subscribers have the option to instantly generate their own contact lists and export them into spreadsheets for further use—a great alternative to high cost list broker services.

ACCESS TO CURRENT LISTINGS FOR...

Banks and Depository Institutions
- Domestic and savings banks
- Foreign banks and branches
- Foreign bank representative offices
- Trust companies
- Credit unions

Non-Depository Institutions
- Bond rating companies
- Collection agencies
- Credit card companies
- Financing and loan companies
- Trustees in bankruptcy

Investment Management Firms, including securities and commodities
- Financial planning / investment management companies
- Investment dealers
- Investment fund companies
- Pension/money management companies
- Stock exchanges
- Holding companies

Insurance Companies, including federal and provincial
- Reinsurance companies
- Fraternal benefit societies
- Mutual benefit companies
- Reciprocal exchanges

Accounting and Law
- Accountants
- Actuary consulting firms
- Law firms (specializing in finance)

Major Canadian Companies
- Key financial contacts for public, private and Crown corporations

Associations
- Associations and institutes serving the financial services sector

Financial Technology & Services
- Companies involved in financial software and other technical areas.

Access even more content online:
Government and Publications
- Federal, provincial and territorial contacts
- Leading publications serving the financial services industry

 For more information please contact Grey House Publishing Canada
Tel.: (866)-433-4739 or (416) 644-6479 Fax: (416) 644-1904 | info@greyhouse.ca | www.greyhouse.ca

Services financiers au Canada

Une couverture sans pareille de l'industrie des services financiers canadiens

Grâce à plus de 30 000 organisations et renseignements commerciaux rares, *Services financiers du Canada* est la source la plus à jour de noms et de coordonnées de professionnels, de membres de la haute direction, de gestionnaires de portefeuille, de conseillers financiers, de fonctionnaires et de représentants élus de l'industrie.

Services financiers du Canada intègre les plus récentes modifications à l'industrie afin de vous offrir les détails les plus à jour au sujet de chaque entreprise, notamment le nom, le titre, l'organisation, les numéros de téléphone et de télécopieur, le courriel et l'adresse du site Web. Servez-vous de la base de données en ligne et raffinez votre recherche selon le symbole, le revenu, l'année de création, les immobilisations, le type de propriété ou le nombre d'employés.

DES INDEX PUISSANTS VOUS AIDENT À TROUVER LES RENSEIGNEMENTS FINANCIERS ESSENTIELS DONT VOUS AVEZ BESOIN.

C'est avec l'utilisateur en tête que Services financiers au Canada a été conçu; il contient des listes catégorisées et quatre index faciles d'utilisation :

Alphabétique—les organisations financières apparaissent en ordre alphabétique, selon le nom de l'entreprise.

Géographique—les institutions financières sont détaillées par ville.

Nom de directeur—tous les agents, directeurs et cadres supérieurs sont classés en ordre alphabétique, selon leur nom de famille.

Classe d'assurance—toutes les entreprises selon leur type d'assurance.

Passez moins de temps à préparer des listes, à faire des recherches ou à chercher des contacts et des courriels. Que vous soyez intéressé à contacter un avocat en droit des affaires au sujet de projets conjoints internationaux et nationaux, que vous ayez besoin de générer une liste des banques étrangères au Canada ou que vous souhaitiez communiquer avec la Bourse de Toronto, *Services financiers au Canada* vous permet de trouver toutes les données dont vous avez besoin.

OFFERT EN FORMAT PAPIER OU EN LIGNE – UN ACCÈS RAPIDE ET FACILE À TOUS LES RENSEIGNEMENTS DONT VOUS AVEZ BESOIN!

Offert sous couverture rigide ou en format électronique grâce au Web, Services financiers du Canada donne invariablement un accès instantané aux personnes et aux faits dont vous avez besoin. Si la version imprimée est vérifiée et mise à jour annuellement, des changements continus sont apportés mensuellement à la base de données en ligne. Servez-vous de la version en ligne afin de circonscrire vos recherches grâce à des champs spéciaux de l'index comme le nom de l'organisation ou son type, le sujet, l'emplacement, le nom de la personne-ressource ou son titre et le code postal.

Créez vos propres listes! Les abonnés au service en ligne peuvent générer instantanément leurs propres listes de contacts et les exporter en format feuille de calcul pour une utilisation approfondie – une solution de rechange géniale aux services dispendieux d'un commissionnaire en publipostage.

ACCÉDEZ AUX LISTES ACTUELLES...

Banques et institutions de dépôt
- Banques nationales et d'épargne
- Banques étrangères et leurs succursales
- Bureaux des représentants de banques étrangères
- Sociétés de fiducie
- Coopératives d'épargne et de crédit

Établissements financiers
- Entreprises de notation des obligations
- Agences de placement
- Compagnies de carte de crédit
- Sociétés de financement et de prêt
- Syndics de faillite

Sociétés de gestion de placements, y compris les valeurs et marchandises
- Entreprises de planification financière et de gestion des investissements
- Maisons de courtage de valeurs
- Courtiers en épargne collective
- Entreprises de gestion de la pension/de trésorerie
- Bourses
- Sociétés de portefeuille

Compagnies d'assurance, fédérales et provinciales
- Compagnies de réassurance
- Sociétés fraternelles
- Sociétés de secours mutuel
- Échanges selon la formule de réciprocité

Comptabilité et droit
- Comptables
- Cabinets d'actuaires-conseils
- Cabinets d'avocats (spécialisés en finance)

Principales entreprises canadiennes
- Principaux contacts financiers pour les sociétés de capitaux publiques, privées et de la Couronne

Les associations et Technologie et services financiers

Accès à plus de contenu en ligne: Gouvernement et Publications
- Personnes-ressources aux paliers fédéral, provinciaux et territoriaux
- Principales publications qui desservent l'industrie des services financiers

 Pour obtenir plus d'information, veuillez contacter **Grey House Publishing Canada**
par tél. : 1 866 433-4739 ou 416 644-6479 par téléc. : 416 644-1904 | info@greyhouse.ca | www.greyhouse.ca

Major Canadian Cities
Compared & Ranked

New edition with 2021 census data!

Major Canadian Cities provides the user with numerous ways to rank and compare 50 major cities across Canada. All statistical information is at your fingertips; you can access details about the cities, each with a population of 100,000 or more. On Canada's Information Resource Centre (CIRC), you can instantly rank cities according to your preferences and make your own analytical tables with the data provided. There are hundreds of questions that these ranking tables will answer: Which cities have the youngest population? Where is the economic growth the strongest? Which cities have the best labour statistics?

A city profile for each location offers additional insights into the city to provide a sense of the location, its history, its recreational and cultural activities. Following the profile are rankings showing its uniqueness in the spectrum of cities across Canada: interesting notes about the city and how it ranks amongst the top 50 in different ways, such as most liveable, wealthiest and coldest! These reports are available only from Grey House Publishing Canada and only with your subscription to this exciting product!

AVAILABLE ONLINE!

Major Canadian Cities is available electronically via the Web, providing instant access to the facts you want about each city, as well as some interesting points showing how the city scores compared with others.

Use the online version to search statistics and create your own tables, or view pre-prepared tables in pdf form. This can help with research for academic work, infrastructure development or pure interest, with all the data you need in one, modifiable source.

MAJOR CANADIAN CITIES SHOWS YOU THESE STATISTICAL TABLES:

Demographics
- Population Growth
- Age Characteristics
- Male/Female Ratio
- Marital Status

Housing
- Household Type & Size
- Housing Age & Value

Labour
- Labour Force
- Occupation
- Industry
- Place of Work

Ethnicity, Immigration & Language
- Mother Tongue
- Knowledge of Official Languages
- Language Spoken at Home
- Minority Populations
- Education
- Education Attainment

Income
- Median Income
- Median Income After Taxes
- Median Income by Family Type
- Median Income After Taxes by Family Type

Transportation
- Mode of Transportation to Work

For more information please contact Grey House Publishing Canada
Tel.: (866)-433-4739 or (416) 644-6479 Fax: (416) 644-1904 | info@greyhouse.ca | www.greyhouse.ca

Principales villes canadiennes
Comparaison et classement

Nouvelle édition avec les données du recensement de 2021 !

Principales villes canadiennes offre à l'utilisateur de nombreuses manières de classer et de comparer 50 villes principales du Canada. Toute l'information statistique se trouve au bout de vos doigts : vous pouvez obtenir des détails sur les villes, chacune comptant 100 000 habitants ou plus. Dans le Centre de documentation du Canada (CDC), vous pouvez classer instantanément les villes selon vos préférences et créer vos propres tableaux analytiques à l'aide des données fournies. Ces tableaux de classement répondent à des centaines de questions, notamment : quelles villes comptent la population la plus jeune? À quel endroit la croissance économique est-elle la plus forte? Quelles villes présentent les meilleures statistiques en matière de main-d'œuvre?

Un profil de ville offre des renseignements supplémentaires afin de vous donner une idée de son emplacement, de son histoire, de ses activités récréatives et culturelles. Suivent des classements qui démontrent l'unicité de la ville dans un spectre de villes qui se trouvent partout au Canada. Vous trouverez également des remarques intéressantes au sujet de la ville et de son classement parmi les 50 principales villes, par exemple selon celle où il fait le mieux vivre, où se trouvent les plus riches et où il fait le plus froid. Ces rapports sont disponibles uniquement auprès de Grey House Publishing Canada et dans le cadre de votre abonnement à ce produit emballant!

PRINCIPALES VILLES CANADIENNES COMPREND CES TABLEAUX STATISTIQUES :

Données démographiques
- Croissance de la population
- Caractéristiques relatives à l'âge
- Ratio homme/femme
- État matrimonial

Logement
- Type et taille du logement
- Âge et valeur du logement

Main-d'œuvre
- Population active
- Emploi
- Industrie
- Lieu de travail

Ethnicité, immigration et langue
- Langue maternelle
- Connaissance des langues officielles
- Langue parlée à la maison
- Populations minoritaires
- Formation
- Niveau scolaire

Revenu
- Revenu médian
- Revenu médian après impôts
- Revenu médian par type de famille
- Revenu médian après impôts par type de famille

Transport
- Moyen de transport vers le travail

OFFERT EN VERSION ÉLECTRONIQUE!

Principales villes canadiennes est offert en version électronique sur le Web. Vous accédez donc instantanément aux faits dont vous avez besoin pour chaque ville, de même que des éléments intéressants qui illustrent la comparaison entre les villes.

Servez-vous de la version en ligne pour effectuer des recherches parmi les statistiques et créer vos propres tableaux, ou consulter les tableaux déjà prêts en format PDF. Elle peut vous aider dans le cadre de recherches pour des travaux universitaires, pour le développement d'infrastructures ou consultez-la par simple curiosité – autant de données réunies en une source modifiable.

Pour obtenir plus d'information, veuillez contacter Grey House Publishing Canada
par tél. : 1 866 433-4739 ou 416 644-6479 par téléc. : 416 644-1904 | info@greyhouse.ca | www.greyhouse.ca

Cannabis Canada

Cannabis Canada is a one-of-a-kind resource covering all aspects of this growing industry. Featuring a wide-ranging collection of reports and statistics, you'll find everything you need to know about this now-legal marketplace, including need-to-know international information.

This first edition includes the State of the Cannabis Industry 2019, exploring the history of marijuana, current regulations, insightful reports, and listings of upcoming trade shows and conferences.

Readers will also discover the brand new Cannabis Industry Buyer's Guide, featuring everything from Licensed Producers to consulting firms, equipment manufacturers to security firms, and more. All listings include specialized fields that go far beyond name and address, and boast crucial, current key contacts.

ADDITIONAL RESOURCES INCLUDE:

- Industry associations
- Financial and venture capital firms
- Law firms
- Government agencies
- Post-secondary schools
- Healthcare and treatment facilities
- Publications

Rounding out the book are Appendices containing detailed statistics, and multiple Indexes to help you navigate this comprehensive body of work.

A CLOSER LOOK AT WHAT'S INSIDE:

State of the Cannabis Industry 2019—A large, detailed section containing everything from the history of cannabis to current legal regulations. Objective reports on all aspects of the industry are also included, as are listings of Canadian and foreign trade shows and conferences.

Cannabis Industry Buyer's Guide—In-depth company listings covering all essential aspects of the industry. This is your go-to source for crucial contacts you need to expand your business, grow your network, or answer your research questions.

Associations—Everything from professional associations to health organizations, including international bodies essential to the industry.

Finance and Venture Capital—All the information you need on insurance, banking, and industry investment.

Law Firms—Find out which law firms offer services in the cannabis space, right down to specific lawyers' specialties!

Government—Federal and provincial departments and agencies that regulate and oversee the cannabis industry in Canada. This is your source for the best contacts in government.

Education—Colleges, universities and specialized schools that offer or are planning to offer cannabis-related courses.

Health—Locations of specialized health facilities, including mental health and addiction treatment programs across the country.

Publications—Listings of Canadian and foreign magazines, both in print and online, serving members of the cannabis community.

AVAILABLE ONLINE!

The *Canadian Cannabis Guide* is also available online on Canada's Information Resource Centre (CIRC). Thousands of companies and contacts are just a click away! Search by name or type of organization, subject, location, contact name or title and postal code. Export results and create mailing lists with this easy-to-use online database – an essential tool for researchers, students, marketing professionals and industry experts alike.

 For more information please contact Grey House Publishing Canada
Tel.: (866)-433-4739 or (416) 644-6479 Fax: (416) 644-1904 | info@greyhouse.ca | www.greyhouse.ca

Cannabis au Canada

Cannabis du Canada est une ressource unique qui porte sur tous les aspects de cette industrie en pleine expansion. Il comprend des entrées exhaustives ainsi qu'une vaste gamme de rapports et de statistiques : vous y trouverez tout ce qu'il y a à savoir sur ce marché désormais légal, y compris des renseignements à portée internationale.

La première édition inclut le document l'État de l'industrie du cannabis 2019 sur l'histoire de la marijuana, les réglementations en vigueur ainsi que des rapports éclairants et des annonces de salons commerciaux et de congrès à venir.

Les lecteurs découvriront également le tout nouveau guide de l'acheteur de l'industrie du cannabis qui couvre un vaste éventail de sujets : des producteurs autorisés aux sociétés de conseil en passant par les sociétés de sécurité et plus encore. Toutes les entrées comprennent des champs spécialisés qui vont bien plus loin que le nom et l'adresse : elles regorgent de contacts essentiels et actuels.

PARMI LES RESSOURCES SUPPLÉMENTAIRES, MENTIONNONS :

- Associations de l'industrie
- Sociétés financières et de capital de risque
- Cabinets d'avocats
- Agences gouvernementales
- Établissements de soins de santé et de traitement
- Publications

Des annexes avec des statistiques détaillées et plusieurs index vous aident à parcourir cet ouvrage exhaustif.

UN EXAMEN PLUS APPROFONDI DU CONTENU :

L'état de l'industrie du cannabis en 2019—Une section détaillée volumineuse : de l'histoire du cannabis à la réglementation actuelle. S'y trouvent également des rapports objectifs portant sur tous les aspects de l'industrie, des entrées relatives aux salons professionnels ainsi qu'aux conférences, au Canada et à l'étranger.

Guide de l'acheteur—Industrie du cannabis : entrées commerciales exhaustives sur tous les aspects essentiels de l'industrie. Il constitue votre source d'information par excellence de personnes-ressources essentielles à l'expansion de votre entreprise et de votre réseau ou à la recherche de réponses.

Associations—Des associations professionnelles aux organismes de santé, y compris les organismes internationaux essentiels à l'industrie.

Finances et capital-risque—Toute l'information dont vous avez besoin au sujet de l'assurance, des services bancaires et du secteur des placements.

Cabinets d'avocats—Découvrez les cabinets d'avocats qui offrent des services reliés aux enjeux du cannabis, jusqu'aux domaines de spécialité d'avocats précis!

Gouvernement—Les agences et ministères fédéraux et provinciaux qui réglementent et surveillent l'industrie du cannabis au Canada. Cette source vous offre les meilleurs contacts à l'échelle du gouvernement.

Enseignement—Collèges, universités et écoles spécialisées qui offrent des cours ayant trait au cannabis ou qui comptent le faire.

Santé—L'emplacement d'établissements de santé spécialisés, notamment en santé mentale et en programmes de traitement des dépendances, partout au pays.

Publications—Listes de magazines, canadiens et étrangers, imprimés et en ligne, que peuvent consulter les participants du secteur du cannabis.

OFFERT EN LIGNE!

Le *Guide canadien du cannabis* sera également offert en ligne dans le Centre de documentation du Canada (CIRC). Un seul clic vous donne accès à des milliers d'entreprises et de personnes-ressources! Effectuez une recherche par nom ou par type d'organisation, par sujet, par emplacement, par code postal, par personne-ressource ou par titre. Exportez les résultats pour créer des listes d'envoi grâce à cette base de données en ligne conviviale, un outil essentiel tant pour les chercheurs, étudiants, professionnels du marketing que pour les experts de l'industrie.

 Pour obtenir plus d'information, veuillez contacter Grey House Publishing Canada
par tél. : 1 866 433-4739 ou 416 644-6479 par téléc. : 416 644-1904 | info@greyhouse.ca | www.greyhouse.ca

Careers & Employment Canada

Careers & Employment Canada is the go-to resource for job-seekers across Canada, with detailed, current information on everything from industry associations to summer job opportunities. Divided into five helpful sections, this guide contains 10,000 organizations and 20,000 industry contacts to aid in research and jump-start careers in a variety of fields.

ADDITIONAL RESOURCES INCLUDE:

- **Associations**
- **Employers**
  - Arts & Culture
  - Business & Finance
  - Education
  - Environmental
  - Government
  - Healthcare
  - Legal
  - Major Corporations in Canada
  - Telecommunications & Media
  - Transportation
- **Recruiters**
- **Summer Jobs**
- **Career & Employment Websites**
  - National & Regional
  - Industry
  - Topic-Specific
  - Employment Options
  - Clientele
  - Where to Get Resources

AVAILABLE ONLINE!

This content is also available online on Canada's Information Resource Centre (CIRC), where users can search, sort, save and export the thousands of listings available. Please visit www.greyhouse.ca to sign up for a free trial.

Rounding off this guide are 70 pages of reports on the current job market in Canada, a list of industry Awards and Honours, as well as Entry, Executive, and Government Contact indexes for even easier reference. Valuable for employment professionals, librarians, teachers, and job-seekers alike, *Careers & Employment Canada* helps take the strain out of job searching by providing a direct link to the organizations and contacts that matter most.

A CLOSER LOOK AT WHAT'S INSIDE:

Reports on the Job Market—A series of articles on the current job market sourced from Statistics Canada—everything from equity in the workplace to the many ways in which the COVID-19 pandemic has affected the labour market.

Associations—Nearly 800 national associations covering an array of industries and professions.

Employers—Need-to-know companies and organizations broken down into 11 master categories such as Arts & Culture, Education, Government, and Telecommunications & Media.

Recruiters—Top recruiting firms across Canada, organized by national and provincial scope.

Summer Jobs—National and regional summer job opportunities—everything from government agencies to summer camps

Career & Employment Websites—Includes hiring and job board platforms broken down by industry, employment tools, and resources by job type and specialized clientele such as Indigenous, New Canadians, People with Disabilities, Women, and Youth.

 For more information please contact Grey House Publishing Canada
Tel.: (866)-433-4739 or (416) 644-6479 Fax: (416) 644-1904 | info@greyhouse.ca | www.greyhouse.ca

Carrières et emploi Canada

Carrières et emploi Canada est la ressource privilégiée pour les personnes en recherche d'emploi partout au Canada. Elle contient de l'information détaillée et actuelle, des associations de l'industrie aux offres d'emploi d'été. Divisé en cinq sections pratiques, ce guide comprend 10 000 contacts d'organisations et 20 000 d'industrie pour aider à la recherche d'emploi et démarrer des carrières dans divers domaines.

LES RESSOURCES SUPPLÉMENTAIRES COMPRENNENT :

- **Associations**
- **Employeurs**
  - Arts et culture
  - Affaires et finances
  - Formation
  - Environnement
  - Gouvernement
  - Soins de santé
  - Domaine juridique
  - Grandes entreprises au Canada
  - Télécommunications et médias
  - Transport
- **Recruteurs**
- **Emplois d'été**
- **Sites sur les carrières et l'emploi**
  - À l'échelle nationale et régionale
  - Industrie
  - Relatif à un sujet précis
  - Possibilités d'emploi
  - Communauté
  - Où trouver les ressources

OFFERT EN LIGNE!

Ce contenu est également offert en ligne sur le centre de documentation du Canada (CIRC) où les utilisateurs peuvent effectuer des recherches, trier, sauvegarder et exporter des milliers d'entrées disponibles. Veuillez visiter www.greyhouse.ca (en anglais uniquement) pour vous inscrire afin d'en faire un essai gratuit.

À la fin de ce guide, vous trouverez 70 pages de rapports sur le marché de l'emploi actuel au Canada, une liste des prix remis par l'industrie ainsi que des index classés par entrée, direction et contact gouvernemental pour en faciliter davantage la consultation. Outil précieux pour les professionnels de l'emploi, bibliothécaires, enseignants et chercheurs d'emploi, *Carrières et emploi Canada* aide à alléger la recherche d'emploi en offrant un lien direct avec les organisations et personnes-ressources plus essentielles que jamais.

UN EXAMEN PLUS APPROFONDI DU CONTENU :

Rapports sur le marché de l'emploi—Une série d'articles sur le marché du travail actuel provenant de Statistiques Canada : de l'équité en milieu de travail aux divers impacts de la pandémie de la COVID-19 sur le marché de l'emploi.

Associations—Près de 800 associations nationales portant sur une gamme d'industries et de professions.

Employeurs—Les entreprises et organisations essentielles, divisées en 11 catégories principales comme les arts et la culture, l'éducation, le gouvernement, les télécommunications et les médias.

Recruteurs—Les principales agences de recrutement partout au Canada, selon leur portée nationale et provinciale.

Emplois d'été—Les occasions d'emploi d'été, à l'échelle nationale et régionale; des agences gouvernementales aux camps d'été.

Sites Web professionnels et d'emplois—Comprend les plateformes d'embauche et d'offres d'emploi, divisées par industrie, outils d'embauche et les ressources par type d'emploi et communautés précises, notamment les Autochtones, nouveaux Canadiens, personnes handicapées, femmes et jeunes.

 Pour obtenir plus d'information, veuillez contacter Grey House Publishing Canada
par tél. : 1 866 433-4739 ou 416 644-6479 par téléc. : 416 644-1904 | info@greyhouse.ca | www.greyhouse.ca

Health Guide Canada
An Informative Handbook on Health Services in Canada

Health Guide Canada: An informative handbook on chronic and mental illnesses and health services in Canada offers a comprehensive overview of 107 chronic and mental illnesses, from Addison's to Wilson's disease. Each chapter includes an easy-to-understand medical description, plus a wide range of condition-specific support services and information resources that deal with the variety of issues concerning those with a chronic or mental illness, as well as those who support the illness community.

Health Guide Canada contains thousands of ways to deal with the many aspects of chronic or mental health disorder. It includes associations, government agencies, libraries and resource centres, educational facilities, hospitals and publications. In addition to chapters dealing with specific chronic or mental conditions, there is a chapter relevant to the health industry in general, as well as others dealing with charitable foundations, death and bereavement groups, homeopathic medicine, indigenous issues and sports for the disabled.

Specific sections include:

- Educational Material
- Section I: Chronic & Mental Illnesses
- Section II: General Resources
- Section III: Appendices
- Section IV: Statistics

HEALTH GUIDE CANADA HELPS YOU FIND WHAT YOU NEED WITH THESE VALUABLE SOURCING TOOLS!

Entry Name Index—An alphabetical list of all entries, providing a quick and easy way to access any listing in this edition.

Tabs—Main sections are tabbed for easy look-up. Headers on each page make it easy to locate the data you need.

Create your own contact lists! Online subscribers have the option to instantly generate their own contact lists and export them into spreadsheets for further use—a great alternative to high cost list broker services.

Each listing will provide a description, address (including website, email address and social media links, if possible) and executives' names and titles, as well as a number of details specific to that type of organization.

In addition to patients and families, hospital and medical centre personnel can find the support they need in their work or study. *Health Guide Canada* is full of resources crucial for people with chronic illness as they transition from diagnosis to home, home to work, and work to community life.

PRINT OR ONLINE—QUICK AND EASY ACCESS TO ALL THE INFORMATION YOU NEED!

Available in softcover print or electronically via the web, *Health Guide Canada* provides instant access to the people you need and the facts you want every time. Whereas the print edition is verified and updated annually, ongoing changes are added to the web version on a regular basis. The web version allows you to narrow your search by using index fields such as name or type of organization, subject, location, contact name or title and postal code.

 For more information please contact Grey House Publishing Canada
Tel.: (866)-433-4739 or (416) 644-6479 Fax: (416) 644-1904 | info@greyhouse.ca | www.greyhouse.ca

Guide canadien de la santé
Un manuel informatif au sujet des services en santé au Canada

Le *Guide canadien de la santé : un manuel informatif au sujet des maladies chroniques et mentales de même que des services en santé au Canada* donne un aperçu exhaustif de 107 maladies chroniques et mentales, de la maladie d'Addison à celle de Wilson. Chaque chapitre comprend une description médicale facile à comprendre, une vaste gamme de services de soutien particuliers à l'état et des ressources documentaires qui portent sur diverses questions relatives aux personnes qui sont aux prises avec une maladie chronique ou mentale et à ceux qui soutiennent la communauté liée à cette maladie.

Le *Guide canadien de la santé* contient des milliers de moyens pour composer avec divers aspects d'une maladie chronique ou d'un problème de santé mentale. Il comprend des associations, des organismes gouvernementaux, des bibliothèques et des centres de documentation, des services d'éducation, des hôpitaux et des publications. En plus des chapitres qui portent sur des états chroniques ou mentaux, un chapitre traite de l'industrie de la santé en général; d'autres abordent les fondations qui réalisent des rêves, les groupes de soutien axés sur le décès et le deuil, la médecine homéopathique, les questions autochtones et les sports pour les personnes handicapées. Les sections incluent

- Matériel didactique
- Section I : Les maladies chroniques ou mentales
- Section II : Les ressources génériques
- Section III : Les annexes
- Section IV : Les statistiques

Chaque entrée comprend une description, une adresse (y compris le site Web, le courriel et les liens des médias sociaux, lorsque possible), les noms et titres des directeurs de même que plusieurs détails particuliers à ce type d'organisme.

Les membres du personnel des hôpitaux et des centres médicaux peuvent trouver, au même titre que parents et familles, le soutien dont ils ont besoin dans le cadre de leur travail ou de leurs études. Le *Guide canadien de la santé* est rempli de ressources capitales pour les personnes qui souffrent d'une maladie chronique alors qu'elles passent du diagnostic au retour à la maison, de la maison au travail et du travail à la vie au sein de la communauté.

OFFERT EN FORMAT PAPIER OU EN LIGNE — UN ACCÈS RAPIDE ET FACILE À TOUS LES RENSEIGNEMENTS DONT VOUS AVEZ BESOIN!

Offert sous couverture souple ou en format électronique grâce au web, le *Guide canadien de la santé* donne invariablement un accès instantané aux personnes et aux faits dont vous avez besoin. Si la version imprimée est vérifiée et mise à jour annuellement, des changements continus sont apportés mensuellement à la base de données en ligne. Servez-vous de la version en ligne afin de circonscrire vos recherches grâce à des champs spéciaux de l'index comme le nom de l'organisation ou son type, le sujet, l'emplacement, le nom de la personne-ressource ou son titre et le code postal.

LE GUIDE CANADIEN DE LA SANTÉ VOUS AIDERA À TROUVER CE DONT VOUS AVEZ BESOIN GRÂCE À CES OUTILS DE REPÉRAGE PRÉCIEUX!

Répertoire nominatif — une list alphabétique offrant un moyen rapide et facile d'accéder à toute liste de cette edition.

Onglets — les sections principals possèdent un onglet pour une consultation facile. Les notes en tête de chaque page vous aident à trouver les données voulues.

Créez vos propres listes! Les abonnés au service en ligne peuvent générer instantanément leurs propres listes de contacts et les exporter en format feuille de calcul pour une utilisation approfondie – une solution de rechange géniale aux services dispendieux d'un commissionnaire en publipostage.

 Pour obtenir plus d'information, veuillez contacter Grey House Publishing Canada par tél. : 1 866 433-4739 ou 416 644-6479 par téléc. : 416 644-1904 | info@greyhouse.ca | www.greyhouse.ca

THE FACTS FOUND FAST!

Tap into FP Corporate Surveys and access all the facts and figures you need to make better informed decisions.

Covering over 6,300 publicly traded Canadian companies, FP Survey - Industrials and FP Survey - Mines & Energy are loaded with financial and operational information. Discover companies' financial results, capital and debt structure, key corporate developments, major shareholders, directors and executive officers, subsidiaries and more!

The ideal complement, FP Survey - Predecessor & Defunct, provides a comprehensive record of changes to Canadian public corporations dating back almost 90 years.

FP Corporate Surveys are completely unbiased, current and credible - make your investment decisions based on the facts.

ALL THE IN-DEPTH INFORMATION THAT YOU NEED – ALL IN ONE PLACE

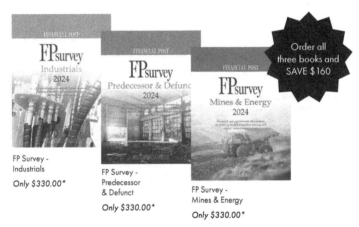

FP Survey - Industrials
Only $330.00*

FP Survey - Predecessor & Defunct
Only $330.00*

FP Survey - Mines & Energy
Only $330.00*

Order all three books and SAVE $160

*Plus shipping and applicable taxes

3 Easy Ways to Order

Phone: 1.866.433.4739 • Fax: 416.644.1904 • Email: info@greyhouse.ca

To Order: Toll Free Tel 1.866.433.4739 • Fax 416.644.1904

Financial Post Fixed Income Books are owned by Financial Post Data, a division of Postmedia Network Inc., and are exclusively printed and distributed by Grey House Publishing Canada.

Make Smarter Investment Decisions

FP Advisor
The ultimate online investment and research tool

As the most trusted and reliable source of corporate data, FP Advisor provides detailed information about public and private companies across Canada, archival financial data, useful analytical and lead generation tools, and more—all in one convenient place.

FP Advisor includes:

Corporate Snapshots	Historical Reports	Dividends
Corporate Surveys	Industry Reports	New Issues
Corporate Analyzer	Predecessor & Defunct	Fixed Income
Investor Reports	Mergers & Acquisition	Directory of Directors

 "FP Advisor is a very important source of information for us. We rely extensively on Predecessor & Defunct and Mergers & Acquisitions to track companies over time. Historical Reports include valuable current operations and ownership details that can be difficult to find elsewhere."
Kathy West, Head, Winspear Business Library, University of Alberta

Get a free trial today!
fpadvisor@postmedia.com | legacy-fpadvisor.financialpost.com